STUDIES ON THE HOLOCENE, PALYNOLOGICAL,PALAEOBOTANICAL AND PALAEOENVIRONMENTAL ASPECTS WITH REFERENCE TO SITES IN NAGPUR DISTRICT, MAHARASHTRA, INDIA

Sharayu D. Sathe

Lulu Publications, North Carolina, USA

© Author

Sharayu D. Sathe

Associate Professor and HOD,
Department of Plant Science
Abasaheb Garware College , Pune 411004. India

December 2011

Published by

Lulu Publications, North Carolina, USA

ISBN: 978-1-300-50070-4

This Book is Dedicated to *Bhartratna* Dr.B.R. Ambedkar

And

Late Dr. K.R. Pandit . Reader, Dept of Botany , University of Pune

CONTENTS

ACKNOWLEDGMENT

I would like to acknowledge that the research for this thesis was carried out while employed at the Botany Dept., Abasaheb Garware college, Pune and I would like to express my thanks towards the Principal of my college Dr.A.S. Inamdar, for giving me the permission to carry on the research, and for all the moral support he had provided during all these years.I am enourmously greatful to Dr.Chaugule B.B.(The HOD, Dept. of Botany, UoP) for extending all kinds of support and cooperation,So also Dr.Shitole M.G.(Ex-HOD ,Dept of Botany, UoP), and Dr.Shirke for helping in identification of plants.

The research was made possible by the co-operation and hospitality of the people of Deccan college, Pune, to whome I am very greatful. I would like to thank the Ex-Directors Prof. Sharma, Dr.Pathan and the present Director Prof.Paddaiya for granting permission to undertake this study.

It is a great pleasure to acknowledge to great extent on which this investigation has dependent upon, the work of my Guru Prof. Kajale M.D. with sediments, past vegetation history, Archaeobotony, Botany, Palaeobotany, Palynology, Palaeopalynology and many other related areas. I am greatly influenced and could receive his support and relay on his foresight, enterprise, and encouragement. I wish to take this opportunity to express my thanks to my Co- Guide Prof. S.Y. Kamble who has provided much help and support and for many fruitful discussions regarding the contemporary floristic studies throughout my research. I am thankful to him for examining part of the plant assemblage and for valuable suggestions, and critical comments on the taxonomy of certain taxa in the study area.

My deepest gratitude is extended to Prof. Rajguru S.N. for associating us to join the important field work in the study area to teach me the basics of Geology, Geomorphology, Sedimentology, Hydrology, Land formations and many other crutial aspects of this research work. I am thankful to the researchers, authors of books, publishers, editors, whose publications have helped me in making out the text of the thesis. I am thankful to my elders whose continuous support and inspiration led me to complete this work. I am grateful to my husband Mr. Devanand H.Sathe and my son Sumit for their perseverance, constant support, and all the help.

Sharayu D. Sathe

December 2011

1

Introduction to Quaternary Palynology

INTRODUCTION

Palaeopalynology is concerned with the study of fossil pollen and spores that have been extracted from the past sediment deposits. Hyde and Williams (1944) originally introduced the term palynology to represent aspects related of the study of pollen and spores. Although there are many fields of palynological research, but this thesis will devote its discussion to only one of them known as "Palaeopalynology".

Pollen analysis is a sub field within the discipline of palynology that is directly concerned with the reconstruction of past environments through the recovery, identification and statistical analysis of preserved fossil pollen grains. This study is possible because the outer wall of pollen grain and spore contain a very durable compound called sporopollenin which is composed of an oxidative co-polymer of carotenoid and carotenoid esters (Brooks and Shaw, 1968;Shaw,1971;Brook,1971). Because of its great durability and resistance to destruction by most types of weathering agents, pollen grains have been recovered from sediments of great antiquity. Fossil pollen has been recovered from sediments as old as Pennsylvanion, > 300 million years old. Fossil vascular plant spores have been recovered from Silurian deposits over 400 million years old and fungal and algae spores have been found in sediments over a billion years old. Although fossil pollen and spores from any of these deposits can be used as a basis for attempting palaeoenvironmental reconstruction, the thesis here is confined to the study of late Quaternary period from the Mansar region of central India since their records are of special interest to archaeologist and ecologist working with modern floral studies. Even though pollen analysis was first developed in the early 1900 s, its full potential as a research tool is only now being realized (Brayant JR., 1978)

Today the scope of pollen analysis is continuously expanding and has been subdivided into numerous specialized divisions, many of which are devoted to some aspects of palaeovegetation reconstruction such as past climate and vegetational changes .The work aims at understanding the techniques of pollen analysis for the reconstruction of palaeoenvironmental data from the relatively less studied Vidharba region of central India.

Various studies were carried out in central India during the last three decades that has provided an excellent picture of the human adaptation to changing environments. Here Considerable multidisciplinary research involving mapping of quaternary formations, locating and excavating archaeological sites for the construction of geological and archaeological sequences, laboratory analysis

1

of sediments, radiometric dating of geological deposits and collection of ethanographic data on hunting gathering and agricultural populations, have been undertaken, in recent times.

The study of palaeo- environmental phenomena in central India constitutes a key aspect of past global changes in India. A better understanding of past changes in the earth's climate system is significant for us to improve our ability to understand future trends of global change under the influence of anthropogenic activity. This study also rests on geological investigations of the area.

The effects of human activity on natural environmental changes over the last 3,000 years have also been a significant factor. This is especially important for the prediction of future climate and environmental changes in Asia. Quaternary palaeopalynological research has received a great importance with the increase in the number of palynological discoveries, made over the last three decades, for example work by Vishnu Mittre(1964), Singh (1971), Agarwal (1987) , Sharma and Gupta (1984) and Kajale (1996) are noteworthy to name a few. There is a remarkable change in the pattern of documentation of the microfossil assemblages which display an increasing attention towards the methods of recovery , analysis and formation of palaeopalynological records and evaluating the same. With the Incorporation of recent advances, it has been possible to understand and evaluate diversity , community ecology and evolution in ancient ecosystems which has made palaeoenvironmental studies more meaningful. It is now widely appreciated that an understanding of the earth's past climatic & environmental variability is an important component for climatic modeling studies aimed at predicting changes (Gupta, 1988; Tara et al.2001).

It is admitted on all hands that climate is one of the most important factors in controlling the origin, development and decline of human cultures as it governs to a considerable degree the organic resources of a region and related human activity. Thus the reconstruction of past climate is important not only to the archaeologists but also to researchers of various other disciplines as well. In this context the study of lacustrine sediments is particularly important as these sediments are better preserved and stratified and can produce better chronological controls on the evidence collected (Robert, 1993)

Holocene climate change has shaped natural communities and the development of human culture. Understanding these changes leads us to a better understanding of our own history, and makes us aware that the contingency of history applies to cultural as well as to organism evolution. Although our knowledge of plant types in our area has improved ,only a considerably small fraction of pollen types are identifiable to species level. Tracing the interaction of humans, climate, and natural communities of the Vidarbha region of Maharashtra throughout the late Holocene is just beginning. Traditional study in plant sciences have helped us in understanding the type of adaptations and habitats of extinct species and throw light on their probable position in the evolutionary history. Palaeobotanical, Palaeoenvironmental, Palynological studies and biogeographic explanations are imperative for a better understanding of the various problems faced by Botanists.(Venkatchala,1986.) The significance of microfossils, as a source of environmental reconstruction, their distribution and preservation has effectively brought out a comprehensive picture of the Holocene flora in India (Singh,1988).

The study of past communities from the microfossils records represent a major step towards the reconstruction of the past ecosystem. Such reconstructions require knowledge about the ecological requirements & tolerances of the species and community involved. These areas have become the focal point of multidisciplinary research for more than a century. It is in this context that the recent discoveries of several fossil bearing sites in the Vidarbha , Marathwada region, assumes great importance for palaeobiogeographical distribution & possible causes of extinction of many plants during the early Quaternary .(Mahajan,and Mahabale 1973).

Such phenomena enable palynologist to reconstruct the past vegetation history and to interpret the depositional environment in terms of the present day known ecological processes. Aided by the palynological data, the riddles of palaeoecology, palaeoenvironment, palaeophytogeography, biostratigraphic correlation, dating of ages etc. can be established based on the depositional pattern of the fossil pollen grains and spores.

Pollen analysis therefore is an extremely powerful tool for the investigation of floristic and climatic changes that took place in the recent past i.e. Quaternary. Precise dating to explore vegetation history may be obtained by employing radiocarbon dating.

Several factors are considered to reconstruct the quaternary palaeoenvironment of a particular region through pollen analysis. They include plant habit, dispersal, and pollination mechanism of plants, meteorological condition including temperature, wind speed, relative humidity and rainfall, influence of glaciation etc. It is fairly well known that the differential preservation of sediments and the destruction of pollen grains and spores, among others due to microbial action and oxidation play important roles to understand the nature of depositional environment (Deotare 1995).   In some cases there could be over representation or under representation of particular pollen types depending upon the pollinating agents, pollen productivity etc.The vegetation pattern generated by the climatic diversity is briefly reviewed. For the Quaternary period palynology has played a key role in reconstructing climatic and vegetational history.But sometimes the botanical markers selected are not filed indicators of climate.(Meher- Homji 1994).Thus along with fossil microflora,focus should also be given to other aspects like 14C dating, geology, Geomorphology,Sediment analysis,Biogeochemical formations in the sediments,Megafossils, Magnetic susceptibility ,Climatic conditions etc. Such multidisciplinary study has enabled us to draw a conclusion about the past vegetation

Applications of palynology and palaeopalynology

Palynology is a science with multifold applications. Advances of this science have enhanced its application potential to the extent that it comes no more now within the limited framework of botanical or geological sciences but enjoy an independent status. providing fertile grounds for the cross fertilization of varied scientific pursuits. Some important fields are outlined.

Palaeoclimate and Vegetational history

Pollen analysis of sedimentary samples helps us to reconstruct pollen diagrams, which provide a picture of the past vegetation of the area. As pollen grains are indicators of species components in a vegetation, dominance or absence of pollen grains in pollen diagram can be correlated to deduce a general picture of dominant habitats prevailed during a particular period like the distributional pattern of forest type, scrub elements or components in a grass land vegetation and so on. Changes in palynostratigraphy normally correspond to changes in vegetational succession. Interpretations of data gained help us to understand the origin, age and vegetational history of forests (Faegri and Iversen 1975; Vishnu-Mittre and Gupta 1972; Godwin, 1975; Lamb, 1977,1984; Bhattacharya and Chanda, 1988).

Vegetation reacts appropriately to changes in temperature and other related ecological factors. It is not very difficult to reconstruct climatic history, as vegetation is a definite indicator of climate. Increase in temperature provides favourable atmosphere for thermophilous species and helps them spreading and dominating such areas, which is reversed by a decrease in temperature and consequently giving way for the emergence of species suitable to low temperature. If the climatic requirements of species identified from the fossil pollen spectra are known, knowledge can be extended from mere temperature factor to other related ecological factors. Presence of tree species favoring tropical humid climate indicates the occurrence of heavy rain fall in the area because temperature and precipitation are interdependent (Rao and Ramanujam, 1982; Raghubanshi et al 1991.) After having known the Climatic factors, palaeoenvironment can well be outlined; more accurately known so, when supplemented with data from geology, atmospheric physics and radiocarbon dating. Information gathered from fossil pollen grains have made possible the reconstruction of not only past vegetation but also the relationship of 'vegetation' to 'climatic changes' and finally the reconstruction of palaeoenvironment for many localities and phytogeographical zones (Godwin, 1960; Nair, 1960; Gupta, 1981; Vishnu-Mittre and Sharma, 1984; Birks, 1986; Nayar 1984., Singh et al.1974.,Kajale et al, 2001) .

(i)   Tracing the history of plant species:

Distribution of a species changes in response to its immediate environmental conditions and other ecological factors in the region. Study of the distribution of a species in space and time helps to trace the history of the species in relation to the critical factors, which positively or negatively affected its distribution. Palaeopalynological studies of relict species provide information about the period of their dominance and reasons for their dwindling with the passage of time. Through the studies in Quaternary palynology (Godwin 1960) traced the history of weeds in Britain. As regards to tracing the history of plant species.

Pollen characters were employed to track the geographical distribution of the species Argenone mexicana by Nair (1962). Analysis of data from palaeopalynological investigations has proved their bearing on the theory of continental drift (Saad, 1974).

(ii)   Plant evolution based on fossil pollen grains:

Spores and pollen grains manifest parallel development with other major units of plants. They play a decisive role in assessing the origin of angiosperms (Doyle, 1978; Muller, 1984). Observation on the sudden appearance of new types of spores and pollen grains, gradual modification of the existing types and the extinction of such types in sedimentary matrix are found very useful to reach conclusions on the evolutionary aspects of present day plants, when such information are correlated with geological periods.

(iii)   Pollen zones study using Radiocarbon dating:

Pollen zones are distinguished by major pollen changes observed in pollen diagrams. These zones can be radiocarbon dated using the pollen contents in the sediments so as to estimate the age of the zone. Geological time scale so calibrated makes the interpretation; of palynological or other stratigraphical data more scientific and precise. Godwin and associates conducted the first systematic dating of pollen zones in 1957 for postglacial deposits at Scaleby Moss, Cumberland. Now-a-days radiocarbon dating has become an integral part of Quaternary palynoslratigraphic studies to estimate the age of sedimentary deposits (Chanda and Mukherjee, 1969).

(iv)   Archaeology:

A primary objective of archaeological investigation is to reconstruct and explain fully as possible mechanisms and and direction of prehistoric cultural change.one of the formerly peripheral areas of archaeological study now being investigated with increased regularity is the recovery and analysis of fossil pollen (Bryant JR.1978).

Extensive pollen analytical accounts given by Dimbleby (1978,1985) a: regards the different European archaeological sites show the extent to which palynology has become one of the most reliable auxiliaries to Archaeology. Charred archaeological organic remains are mostly dated by pollen analysis and sediments from excavation sites are analyzed for correlation with related information .to gain knowledge on human civilization connected with agriculture and other plant based activities, (Van Zeist, 1955)

Agricultural activities resulted by human settlement in an area influence its environment and such settlements ultimately lead to activities connected with human civilization. Intense palaeopalynological investigations have yielded much information about different aspects of human civilization like the domestication of plants in South and South East Asia (Vishnu-Mittre and Guzder, 1975),), The plant economy of protohistoric and historic times in Madhya Pradesh India (Vishnu-Mittre, 1966), the settlement of early man in North West India (Vishnu-Mitttre1979), the civilization in Harappa (Vishnu-Mittre, 1982), Diet among the Mesolithic hunters and foragers.(Kajale.1996C)

(v)   Biostratigraphy:

Stratigraphy is the study of layered or stratified rocks. It is of great practical value. Correlation of data gathered from local sequence of strata provides clue to the local geological history. The integration of local histories into a regional or worldwide chronological frame work helps us gain knowledge about the geological history of the earth. Palynology is an important parameter in stratigraphy (Grichuk, 1986) and perhaps the only one to rely on in the absence of information from litholog'y, megafossil flora and fauna. Palynostatigraphy carried out for tropical areas by India by Bhattachajya and Chanda (1988), Gupta and Sharma (1982), Vishnu-Mittre and Sharma 1984), are highly reliable sources of information for the stratigraphic studies.

(vi)   Neopaleonology

The diversity and magnitude of Neopaleonology has opened a vast field of palynologial research, both applied and pure, based on Indian fossil as well as extant pollen grains. Angiosperm taxa occurring in India are estimated to be about 20,000 and many among them are reportedly rare and endemic. Study of modern pollen grains helps in identification of palynofacies in the sediments,by comparative study. Thus a reference collection of modern pollen grains is a must while reconstructing the past vegetation.

Aims and objectives of palaeoecological studies.:

The aim of the field investigation reported on here was to carry out pollen analysis with a view to reconstructing the development of natural landscape and history of agriculture in the area – Mansar (Nagpur) .The present investigation into the vegetation history of the lake region, forms part of ongoing palynologidal studies from 1991-2000. The preliminary account of these investigation has been given by Kajale (Pers. Cumm: M.D.Kajale).

So far pollen content studies have mostly been carried out on lake sediments, however, the site like Mansar (Nagpur) has its own inland basin characteristics with respect to pollen deposition , since air , land, and water transported here have dispersed the taxa widely. Therefore, it was important to understand these features .Lithological and biostratigraphic records from Mansar lake sediments provided the best opportunity for a reconstruction of environmental changes in central India. Lakes are excellent repositories of air-borne & especially stream borne materials. It has long been recognized that lake sediments contain a strong record of catchments soils via the input of minerogenic & chemical erossional products. To these may be added a variety of palaeoecological indicators

6

including pollen, fungi, & faunal remains. We were interested in collecting the soil samples from the dried fresh water bodies of the Mansar lake.

Objectives

The present analysis has concerned only a selected portion of information and is made with the most appropriate method for reconstruction of past climates.

This will enable us to extend the sequences to historical time & environmental variations that are reflected by the pollen assemblages.

This work will make its humble contribution toward the better future management of sub humid region, which could only rely on better knowledge of the past, a past which could be revealed by further development of palynological research in sub humid lands.

Strength and understanding of the present work

A key strength of the present work accrues from its multidisiplinary approach and that it has attempted Palaeopalynological, Palaeoecological, Geological, Biogeochemical, Chronological, correlation, using process based approach, coupled with modern floristic study not simplistic interpretation of lithofacies alone. Recent advances in chronological methods like 14C dating and Magnetic susceptibility have been exploited to firmly establish regional chronologies. These efforts have placed the interpretation and understanding of past environmental changes on a much stronger footing, which have enhanced investigations of forcing mechanisms, our ability of science to understand the future changes that are likely to impact upon environment and concern people.

The following information could be possibly inferred from the studies:

Applied sciences:

1)   Improved capacity to unravel human and climatic impact on environmental changes.

2)   Clearer understanding of forcing mechanisms responsible for process changes at key periods in the late Quaternary. especially during Holocene.

3)   Clearer understanding of contrast in environment and vegetations, reducing reliance on over general global models and extrapolation of data from a limited number of locations.

4)   Advanced knowledge of the environment- vegetation- society linkages in past and present vegetation changes, thereby informing model and predictions of future changes and their relation to local systems, including: detailed understanding of contrasts and comparisons from the study area in timing and nature of major environmental changes and causes of these contrasts especially in climate forcing mechanisms and the roles of specific human activities as contributions to vegetational changes.

Identification of human vs. natural causes of past vegetational changes and production of list of indicators for identifying the nature and causes of changes particularly the prevalence of process and surface changes.

Understanding of past human relationship with environmental and vegetation changes in study area. This has included efforts to establish reasons for different relationships having occurred in different locations and lessons for the future.

As benefits to society:

• Contribution to understanding deforestation, desertification, and future environmental changes affecting vulnerable populations in study area including :

• Marked improvements in the quality of the climatic data inputs for modeling predicted future vegetational and environmental changes. This may improve the capabilities of government and organizations in planning, prepared less for future changes.

• Better understanding of human causes of deforestation during historical and earlier periods and ecosystem management strategies to be adopted.

• By understanding the precise nature of past vegetational changes and susceptibility of this region to specific changes. Future vegetation susceptibility to process and landscape changes. This will enhance predictive capabilities to benefit societies threatened by future global warming and subsequent changes.

• Marked improvement in understanding the role of different process domains in study area and links to forcing mechanisms . This will contribute to predicting future changes in the ecosystem that may occur, permitting necessary action to be taken.

• Significant transfers of information to researchers in less developed areas through collaboration and involvement in the new project, strengthening local knowledge increasing scientific self sufficiency.

• Enhanced understanding ,at global and specific regional level, of the complex factors that have contributed to and will contribute in future to natural environmental changes and Man made environmental change.

Recent development in palaeopalynological researches show that this important issue is both complex and multidimensional . It is not a simple change of shifting vegetational frontiers. It is increasingly recognized that the process of deforestation , which is linked to the complex interaction between human activities in this area and the dynamics of the natural environment. Future predicted anthropogenically induced climate changes are likely to further complicated the rate and nature of the occurrence of vegetational degradation, bringing further risks to populations in such area, food production activities and general environmental security in this area.

We live in the twenty first century ,and the vegetation changes offer many challenges to the societies that live in them. These areas are experiencing, particularly in the developing world, rapid population growth and significant changes in livelihood and attempts to conduct agriculture. These societies are also vulnerable to natural climatic variability, and the vulnerability may be enhanced by the uncertain impact of future climate changes. Changes in climate impact upon the operation of geomorphic and hydrological processes, the occurrence of high magnitude environmental degradation and changes in vegetation cover are so critical to the growing human populations that it is vital to improve our detail understanding of this area and the linkage between specific causes of change and their outcomes in the present day environment.

The above points make it imperative to examine the study area, both as individual entity but also in a holistic manner, in order to prepare a basis for improved predictions of future vegetational and climate change. It was vital to examine a number of key issues in this area as a whole, as well as enhancing our knowledge of past vegetation changes. The present work discussed in this thesis has investigated new issues and brought together a growing body of data in an attempt to seek explanations of differences from the study area, rather than simply describing them. It has also developed an improved understanding of the processes including the role of high magnitude of palaeoclimatic events, the development of carbonates, and inter-play between hydrological processes. Human interactions with the operation of natural processes in the past and present was a key component of investigation.(Soni,2003;Ramkrishnan.2003)

Previous work

Pollen analysis has played a major contribution to the palynological studies in Indian contest . in order to have a summary of the work conducted so far , the information compiled is presented region wise in the global context. As most of the work is carried out by scholars from various geological settings and epochs, a brief summary table of different geological eras is given here for due reference. (Robert,1993).

Late Pleistocene – 20,000 – 10,000 years B.P.

The Pleistocene Prelude – > 10,000 years B.P.

Early Holocene – 10,000 – 5,000 years B.P.

Late Holocene –5,000 - 500 years B.P

Modern time 500 - 0 years B.P.

Quaternary pollen records in India

It was Huntington (1906) who initiated the pollen analysis in India from sediments of pangong lake in ladakh. Later, Wodehouse (1935), De terra and Paterson (1939) worked out palynologically Indian quaternary sediments. The investigations on pollen analysis to establish the quaternary vegetation history palaeoecology, Biostratigraphy and mapping in India have been done adequately. The karewas of Kashmir, Bengal basin and a few other places convey a more or less distinct idea about the divergence of palaeoenvironmental condition, ranging from temperate climate to tropical desert.

The investigations on Quaternary pollen analysis in connection with the vegetation history. So far done in India with greatly diversified floral and ecological distribution are limited in relation to the vastness of the Political Indian subcontinent

As a result unlike North America and North European countries, in India we do not have a comprehensive picture of the Quaternary vegetation history and climate in a chronological sequence.

In Eastern India work on this line has mainly been done in Bengal basin showing chronological history of the mangrove evolution. In North – Eastern India, extensive work has been done is Assam. More extensive work has been done in Northern India mainly in Kashmir valley, Himachal Pradesh and Uttar Pradesh. (Chanda and Bhattacharya,1987).

Rajasthan has been the main point in Western India followed by Gujarat. And finally in Southern India some areas of Nilgiris and coastal Kerala, Karnataka and Tamilnadu have been covered.

The Indian palynologist are working in various universities and institutions to reveal the history of Quaternary vegetation by using pollen analytical method supported in many cases by 14 C dating. It has been adequately demonstrated that different past ecological environments are characterized by diverse topography and floral assemblages.

The assemblages translated into fossil pollen grains and spores in turn indicated the type and character of that particular environment.

The depositional vegetation and environment as already emerged, conveyed a picture of divergence in the characters of past vegetation and palaeoenvironment from place to place in India ranging from tropical, desert, coastal to temperate conditions. This gets reflected in the present distribution of Indian climatic environment with a consequential heterogeneity in the floral distribution.

Maharashtra

So far as eastern Maharashtra ,is concerned very little work has been carried out on Holocene palaeoenvironment except Archaeological work by Nath,1990; Deotare et al.1999; Deotare, 2003). Pollen analysis of coastal region in Bombay (Vishnu – Mittre and Guzder, 1975) revealed sporadic presence of mangrove and allied taxa such as Acanthus illicifolus, Avicennia, Carallia, Chenopods, Excoecaria, Sonneratia, Leguminosae. Caratine et al. (1980) palynologically investigated a 270 m deep profile near Thane, Bombay (Mumbai). The analysis showed poor representation of mangrove elements and abundance of grasses. The occurrence of casuarina pollen from bottom to top of the profile suggest the recent age of sediments.

Rattan and Chandra (1984) investigated recent sediments of the continental shelf off Mumbai of which all the 22 samples had pollen grains of mangrove, tropical evergreen and mixed deciduous type of forest. Pollen of non-arboreal plants and pteridophyte spores were also recorded in huge quantities. It was observed that the samples collected near the coast have yielded more pollen grains. A preliminary palynological study of alluvial sediments around Nirgudsar in the Ghod valley ,upland Maharashtra was undertaken by Kajale and Rajguru. 1976;Vishnu M.,and Gupta 1976).

A methodological approach had been implemented to improve the pollen recovery from minerogenic sediments by Deotare, (1995).On the same line(Deotare and Kajale,1996) it was proved that the microfossils were preserved better in association with the copper objects from Megalithic sites in Maharashtra. Analysis of some Charophyta was undertaken (Bhatia and Mannikeri, 1976) from the Deccan intertrappean beds near Nagpur, central India. Nath extensively studied archaeology of Wardha and Wainganga divide in 1990.

The archaeological site near the Mansar lake, Nagpur, Maharashtra was excavated by Joshi and Sharma A.K, (2000). Effect of climatic and environmental Changes on human has been a controversial subject. In India we examine the evidence of environmental change and its effect on human settle settlements. The three regions are, Kashmir, Rajasthan and Ganga valley. Much of the work in palaeopalynology and palaeoecology along west coast in marine sediments in Maharashtra is contributed by Kumaran. et al (2001, 2004, 2004a, 2004b, 2005) Limaye (2004, 2007); Shindikar (2004, 2006).

Pollen analysis of coastal region in Bombay (Vishnu-Mittre and Guzder, 1975) revealed sporadic presence of mangrove and allied taxa such as Acanthus illidfolius, Avicennia, Carallia, Chenopods, Excoecaria, Sonneratia, Legu-minosae, Myrtaceae, etc.Study of mangrove vegetation with respect to palynological study and recent history was undertaken to reveal their importance in coastal ecosystems.(Caratini et al 1980; Shindikar 2006)Ratan and Chandra(1984) have carried out palynological investigations from the recent sediments of the continental shelf off, Bombay. Caratini et al. (1980) palynologically investigated a 270 m deep profile near Thane, Bombay. The analysis showed poor represen¬tation of mangrove elements and abundance of grasses. The occurrence of Casuarina pollen from bottom to top of the profile suggests the recent age of the sediments.

Ratan and Chandra (1984) investigated recent sediments of the continental shelf off Bombay, of which all the 22 grab samples had recorded pollen grains of mangrove, tropical evergreen and mixed deciduous type of forest. Pollen of non-arboreal plants and pteridophyte spores were also recorded in huge quantities. It was observed that the samples collected from near the coast have yielded more pollen grains. For Kashmir and Rajasthan we have adequate climatic information for the Holocene but for the Ganga valley we have limited data Rajasthan witnessed the growth and decline of the first urbanization represented by the Harappa culture. The Ganga valley went through the second urbanization marked by the advent of Iron age. In Kashmir however it was not the rainfall that mattered but the temperature.(Gupta, 1992).

Kashmir

The climatic sequence of Kashmir and its relation with the human habitations has studied and The period C.18000 BP is marked by a palace sol and B.C values indicate dominance of thermophilous plants over conifers. Both pollen spectra from the Anchar Lake and the first palaeosol indicate climatic amelioration in the valley the next climatic amelioration of C. 1800 BP is associated with the emergence of large kushan habitation and that of early medieval warming with the rise of Hindu Kingdom of Lalitaditya and Avanti varman and the great sun temple that they built (,. Agrawal 1987 ,Agrawal et al 1989). The study of vegetation history and palaeoenvironment of Ningle Nullah,Lower Karewa, Kashmir ,have inferred that the vegetation enjoyed temperate and humid climate.(Gupta and Sharma,1992).

The results obtained from the Baltal pollen profile ,from Karewas relict lake sediments ,dating back to c 3.5 M yr.infer palaeoclimatic changes in the valley of Kashmir,India during mid Pleistocene,representing cold phases each alternating with warm oscillations.(Dodia,1988)

Himachal Pradesh

The pollen analytical investigations of modern as well as post glacial sediments from Parasram Tal of Himachal pradesh suggested overall dominance of Chirpine Okes together with other broad leaved taxa indicative of warm temperate and humid climatic conditions in late Quaternary period, dated 3140 yr.B.P.(Sharma,1985.)

Rajasthan

The Thar desert today marks this area. Agrawal et al have worked out an outline of the Quaternary climatic history of Rajasthan and according to him Thar Desert came in to existence about 200 k yr.He thought that man – environment relationship in Rajasthan is determined by three main factors. Change in rainfall, Change in palaeoclimate caused by neo-tectonics and limited capacity of semi arid ecology to sustain large sedentary populations. (Agrawal et al .1995) Singh et al. (1974) had carried out pollen studied on the cores raised from the saline lakes of Didwana, Lunka ransan and Sambhar in Rajasthan.

The summer monsoon is essentially the only rain in northern India, but in mid Holocene time there was 'also' considerable winter rainfall." These climatic inferences were based on rain- sensitive pollen spectra.

Wasson et al. (1983) carried out extensive geochemical and sedimentological studies at Didwana. They inferred that the deepest water conditions in the entire sequence were indicated soon after 6 k yr . Thus confirming the climatic pattern indicated by pollen studies. It has been noted that the role of climate and environment in affecting habitations, especially the Harappan culture (Singh 1971).

Thus is Rajasthan its not only the changing precipitation that affects habituation but also the changing loyalties of the rivers and the also the changing loyalties of the rivers and the sustainability thresholds of semi arid ecology to allow large sedentary populations for long period of time. All these trends are superimposed on each other in Rajasthan

The history of post-glacial vegetation and palaeoecology of the Rajasthan desert were worked out on the basis of fossil pollen curves from the following regions:

Singh et al. (1974) investigated the vegetational history of the Rajasthan desert based on four pollen sequences, one each from Lunkaransar Salt lake under arid belt, Sambhar and Didwana Salt lakes under semi-arid belt and Pushkar fresh water lake under semi-humid belt. The whole vegetational history of Rajasthan could be grouped into six phases (I - VI) of which all but phase I belonged to Holocene Period (Gupta 1974).

Vishnu-Mittre and Gupta (1976) contradicted the conclusions of Singh et al. (1974) by his contention that the humid belts of Sambhar, Didwana and Lunkaransar areas remained the same as it is now. Lunkaransar, according to them, is driest, and Sambhar is the least dry .It was noted that the behaviour of Cyperaceae and Artemisia was found to be inversely related at the two sites and in Didwana the declining Artemisia pollen curve remained enigmatic.

The gradual formation of Calligonum-Capparis series in the vicinity of Lunkaransar and of Capparis - Prosopis- Acacia and Euphorbia association in the vicinity of Sambar lake suggested an increase of aridity, spread of aolian sand and extension of the dune formation activity. This large scale desertification of Rajasthan was not only infested by the climatic factor but also by the increasing biotic influence like human interference and over-grazing .

So from the pollen analytical study of the Rajasthan desert during the last 10000 years it is revealed that there was an increasing trend towards dryness until 5000 years ago. Between 5000 to 3000 years ago climate was characterized by optimum warmth, dryness and by high velocity wind and dust storm. The precipitation showed a gradient from the extreme west of the desert to the east. The large-scale desertification was caused by the combined effect of climatic and biotic factors.

The Holocene history of vegetation and climate of fresh water Punlota (Degana) Lake in Eastern Rajasthan ,has revealed that around 9000 yrs B.P. the region had predominantly non arboreal vegetation depicting arid climatic conditions around 4200 yrs B.P. (Sharma et al .2003). Studies of the Aeolian dynamics of the Thar desert, and the lake records of the Thar desert(Singh et al.1974; Wasson et al.1983) have shown that the Holocene climatic changes were significant and there was a broad synchronism in the timing of the changes in the different climatic zones and geomorphic systems.(Mishra and Rajguru, 2001).Palaeoenvironmental studies in western India have demonstrated that during the early to Mid Holocene (8 ka-4ka) ,the climate was relatively humid with intermediate fluctuations and after 4 ka it became semi-arid to arid with less fluctuations. The period between 400 and 900 AD was of reduced settlements in western and central India.

The Indian Thar desert is an extension of the mid- latitude desert belt and is one of the most populated arid regions of the world. A reasonable account of multidisciplinary studies involving disciplines like Geology, geochronology, palynology, stable isotope studies and Archaeology have been carried out during the last 30 years (Singh 1971, Singh et al. 1974; Thomas et al. 1999).

Additionally, detailed Quaternary palaeoenvironmental studies involving lacustral stratigraphy, palynology, geomorphology and archaeology studies etc. in arid core of the Thar desert have unraveled some interesting new data on palaeomonsoon, prehistoric cultures and palaeoenvironmental history (Kajale .1995,1996, Kajale and Deotare 1988, 1989, 1993,1995,1997; Deotare and Kajale 1996, 1999, Deotare 2003;Deotare et al.1999; Kajale et al. 1976,1997, 2001).

Madhya Pradesh

Pollen analysis from Derbokhoh swamp (kusmi),Sidh district (Madhya pradesh) has revealed that around 1500 to 1160 yr.B.P.the diversified tropical deciduous Sal forest constituted of Shorea robusta, Madhuca indica , emblica officinales, Buchnania lanzen etc. occurred in the region under warm and moist climatic condition between 1160-800 yr,B.P. The decline in the Sal forest as well floristic diversity implies that the climate became relatively less moist than before possibly due to weak summer mansoon. Since800 yr.B.P. to present ,the maximum expansion of Sal together with relative better representation of its other associates such as Madhuca indica, Lagerstromia ,Emblica officinales, other Sapotaceae and Adina cordifolia depicted the prevalence of moist climate attributed to strong summer mansoon.

Uttar Pradesh

Tiwari (1993) has discussed the potential of palaeopalynology in high calibre correlation and dating of coal bearing Gondwana sequence of India. Three profiles were studied from the surface samples of the Nainital region namely; Naukuchia Tal, Bhim Tal and Sat Tal. It was demonstrated that the past vegetational pattern was not very different from each other In this regions (Gupta 1977, Gupta and Khandelwal 1982.). From the same region five pollen diagrams were constructed one each from Ram Tal, Sita Tal, Shatrughan Tal and Tarag Tal showing vegetational sequences during last 10,000 years B.P. (Sharma 1992). Three pollen zones are recognized in each pollen diagram on the basis of significant variations in the over all vegetation assemblages which show uniformity in the vegetational sequences.

The late -Quaternary deposits from Naukuchia Tal were initially investigated by Vishnu-Mittre et al. (1967), where a succession between chirpine woods and oak woods was demonstrated. Oaks invaded Chirpine forest and established a mixed Oak forest, eventually leading to a change in climate from dry to wet and humid.The large bottom sediments of Naukuchia Tal were palynologically analyzed (Sharma and Chauhan, 1988). The results reveal the mixed Oak - Chirpine forests along with other broad leaved elements like birch, elm, walnut, willow, Rhododendron, etc. during 4000 yrs. B.P. This association suggests a warm temperate and humid climate. In later part around 1000 yrs. B.P., Chirpine dominated over Oak as a result of less humid climate condition than before. Subsequently, around 600-500 yrs. B.P. grasses along with some cultivation indicators like Artemisia, Plantago- Cheno-Amaranths showed their dominance, which indicates anthropogenic activities in this region. Gupta (1977) has studied the Ganga valley for palacoclimatic data by collecting a pollen sequence from an Oxbow lake in Pratapgarh District of Uttar Pradesh in Ganga valley. He has concluded that – "The climate sequence, as determined from the biostratigraphy of the lake basin has been grouped into four phases. (I – IV) .The general vegetation pattern is rather uniform and is tipped more towards open. Savannah forest with vast of grasslands and a few scattered strands of arboreal vegetation".Development of morphology and soils of the study area in the Ganga plains, according to a more recent study is in conformity with general pattern of climatic amelioration during mid-holocene in all the three regions of Kashmir, Rajasthan and Ganga valley. But it is obvious that in Ganga valley the urbanization processes had to wait till the middle of the first millennium B.C. The monsoonal forests mentioned in the epics as mahavana, which were dark even in the day, could be cleared only after the mass production of iron artifacts which alone made it possible to drain the swamps and clear the dense forests to produce the requisite agricultural surplus which alone could sustain towns and cities. (Stanley and Hait. 2000).Geel, et al. (2001) have investigated Solar forcing (heat exchange) of climate change and a monsoon related cultural shift in western India around 800 cal B.C. In this preliminary paper they have focus on evidence for climate change in India (a dryness crisis), starting around 850 cal B.C. and a cultural shift accordingly.

Based on palynological data from Rajasthan lake deposits, the following climatic sequence for the Holocene period has been reconstructed by Krishnamurthy et al (1981).

Before	8000 BC	Severe aridity
8000	7500 BC	relatively wet
7500	3000 BC	relatively dry
3000	1700 BC	Sudden increase in wetness
1700	1500 BC	Relatively dry
1500	1000 BC	Relatively wet
1000	500 BC	Arid

Based on this data it has been understood that there was a dry phase at the end of the chalcolithic culture around 800 cal B. C in western India. Largescale excavations have revealed various aspects, including socio- economic organizations of settlements. This climatic sequence is probably applicable to the larger semi-arid region of western and central India. (Yasuda and Shinde 2001,2004).

The climate during the late middle and late Pleistocene was semi arid to arid, with several wet episodes. It was hyper arid during the terminal Pleistocene when large scale sand deposition took place and human occupation was considerably reduced spatially and in intensity. Buried sediments in many saline playas like Sambhar, Kuchaman, Didwana, Thob, Malhar and Lunkaransar reveal that around 15,000 yr B.P the climate began to ameliorate and the period from ca. 60,000 to ca 4000 B.P was the wettest. Pollen, laminated black clays indicate perennial fresh water lakes during this period.

Himalaya

The research carried out by Kotlia et al (2004) on the late quaternary tectonics and climate of the central Himalaya of India concludes that an episode of a prominent neotectonic activity on the subsidiary thrusts in the zones of active intracrustal boundary thrust. The Palynological investigations were studied with previously documented late Quaternary climatic changes as recorded in the Ladakh Himalaya and Tibet. Description of late Quaternary flora and fauna has been given by Kotlia et al. (2004) . Based on this data palaeocommunities the palaeoclimate were proposed.The savanna grassland community is represented by Poaceae and large mammals ,the lacustrine community by freshwater gastropods.

Pollen analysis of recent moss cushions in different habitat of the eastern Himalaya (Darjeeling and Sikkim regions) portrays a reasonably accurate record of the extant vegetation in forested areas.(Sharma,2001;Sharma et al 2000)Pollen analysis of a sedimentary profile from Kechipiri Lake located in the Sikkim Himalaya range,have revealed consistent and considerable increase in the herbaceous elements along with the higher number of agricultural pollen , consistent with the present climatic phase of higher precipitation.

Eastern India -Bengal Basin

The Bengal Basin in Holocene period, as a whole, is of sedimentary nature, at the level of 30 m below the surface. The lithochronologic character in vertical as well as horizontal directions is more or less same on both sides of the river Hooghly (Ghosh, 1964). The geochronological sequence of Bengal Basin from Pleistocene to Recent times was investigated by Sengupta (1966), he stated that during early Pleistocene time, shallow marine conditions prevailed only in the deeper parts of the Bengal Basin.

Chanda and Mukherjee (1969) applied 14C dating accompanied by pollen analysis from sediments of Salt Lake and Bagirhat. The floristic compositions recorded from the sediments indicate the existence of a typical swamp type of vegetation along with mangrove in and around Calcutta, similar to the present day vegetation of the Sunderban region of West Bangal. Mukherjee (1972) also constructed pollen diagrams from sediments of Salt Lake from Baidyabati, Belgachia and Bagirhat regiuons of the same region where the vegetation was found to be dominated by mangrove elements about 5000 yrs. B.P.

Vishnu-Mittre and Gupta (1981) reconstructed the palaeovegetation of mid- Palynological studies of several peat profiles Holocene sediments from Sankrail-Jangalpur. The records reviled diatoms of freshwater dating back to 2640±150 yrs. B.P. The Holocene sediments of Sankrail supported the existence of a freshwater environment (Gupta and Khandelwal, 1984, Gupta 1981) palynologically investigated the Holocene sediments from Kolara, Barrackpur, Namkhana and Chaltiya. The results revealed differences in the development of vegetation in all the four parts of basin.

Bengal Basin

Caratini et al. (1980) palynologically investigated six surface samples and two soil profiles, from Kalibhanja Dian island and Talchua village of Brahmani Delta, Orissa respectively. The analysis of surface samples shows partial resemblance with the surrounding vegetation. The profile samples also show the similar results, except for the bottom samples of Talchua profile which has recorded high frequency of mangrove pollen.

Gupta and Yadav (1990) palynologically investigated eight samples from Paradip and Jambu islands. The bottom samples of the pollen diagram of Paradip profile dated to be 500 yrs. B .P. recorded moderate frequency of mangroves with the high values of fresh water influx in deltaic complex which continues till the middle of the profile. The upper part of the profile showed overall dominance of mangrove taxa except at the top of theTaiagram.

West Bengal

D'Costa and Mukherjee (1986) investigated two peat deposits namely, Lopchu and Barasenchal of Darjeeling hill. A total of 35 fern spores were recovered from the deposit, dated to be 3000 yrs. B.P. The profiles were divided into two pollen zones based on the fern spore taxa. It was understood that the two deposits were not co-relatable, except climatically.

Manipur

Roy and Chanda (1988) investigated a late-Quaternary deposit near Loktak lake of Manipur. The profile consisted interbedded black clay. The pollen analysis revealed an admixture of ferns and angiosperms. The profile was divided into three pollen zones. The zone I indicates a relatively cool and humid condition. The zone II showed tropical to sub-tropical forest, while the zone III showed tropical rain forest.

Assam

The late Quaternary vegetation history, Palaeoecology and biostratigraphy of some deposits of Bramhaputra basin, Upper Assam wwre palynologically analysed by Bhattacharya and Chanda (1988). The 14C dating obtained from the profiles suggested a late Quaternary age of the deposits ranging from 12210-17930 yr.B.P. Similarly, twelve fossil angiosperms taxa were described from the Mid tertiary to Quaternary deposits of the subsurface samples from Tinali area of Upper Assam with the aid of palaeopalynology by Mandal and Kumar (2000).

The palynostratigraphy of Balugaon profile in Chilka lake shows the evolutionary pattern of mangrove taxa during 3100 years (Gupta and Khandelwal 1990). In this region pollen/vegetation relation¬ship in different depositional environments like soil, lake bottom mud and lake water samples were also constructed. The relative values of different palynodebris such as fungal spores, microforaminifera, Concentricystis, dinofla-gellates, diatoms, fern spores and pollen grains depicted to the lack of uniformity of the palynodebris in and around Chilka lake, possible due to the underwater channels governing the movement of water both from sea and rivers into the lake. The results revealed the dominance of peripheral mangroves and co -dominance of core mangrove taxa which was found to be incoherent with the present day vegetation in and around Chilka Lake.

A pollen diagram was constructed from a 5.50m thick profile from Balugaon, Chilka Lake dated to 3100 yrs. B.P. to show the recent evolution of mangrove vegetation, North-Eastern India –Assam. Gupta (1971) investigated upper Pleistocene "sediments of Cinnamara in northern Assam.The pollen spectra indicated a sub -tropical vegetation with high precipitates comprising of Dillenia, Ardisia, Cinnamomum, Eurya, Quercus, Syzygium, Ternstroemia, bamboos and various kinds of ferns.

Bhattacharya et al. (1986) constructed a pollen diagram of a 2.30m thick sub-surface peat profile (12210 ± 340 yrs. B.P.) of Tinsukia, upper Assam and divided them into two pollen zones. The Zone I suggests a sub¬tropical/temperate climate comprising of conifers and cold-loving angiosperms and Zone II an open land vegetation dominated by ferns and grasses probably indicating a slightly cooler and humid environment. The deforested condition probably was caused by sharp climatic fluctuations.

Further, the late-Quaternary vegetational history and biostratigraphy of upper Assam were extensively worked out (Bhattacharya 1986, Bhattacharya and Chanda, 1988). Bhattacharya and Chanda (1988) constructed three pollen diagrams from three different locations, viz. Laikajan Padumoni and Lekhapani in upper Assam. Here the pollen diagram was divided into two zones. The Zone I shows sub-tropical to temperate forested condition comprised of Pinus type, Salix, Tsuga, Betula, Carya, Pterocarya, Ardisia etc. The Zone II is characterized by a large number of non-arboreal taxa, showing a deforested and humid condition.

Bhattacharya and Chanda, (1988) inferred that some degrees of climatic fluctuations did occur in Assam during late Quaternary period. Only one peak each of brestation has been found to occur in all the profiles. The forestation phenomenon was generally associated with the decrease in the frequency of grasses and other associated weeds, the pollen diagrams showed that the lower parts were represented by temperate to sub-tropical plants, which tend to disappear in the upper part, perhaps indicating that the climatic condition deteriorated resulting into deforestation. It may be assumed that a primitive agricultural practice existed in more recent time, which is evidenced by the cerelia pollen.

Tripura

The late-Quaternary peat bog deposit in Kalapanya, Tripura, were palynologically analysed (Sarkar et al. 1984). The preliminary results revealed a mixed vegetation comprised of ferns originating from Lygodium, Lepisorus, Sphenomeris, Phymatodes, conifer (Pinus) and angiosperms like Crinum, Mangifera, Fabaceae, Urticaceae, Compositae etc. and a large number of grasses.

Sikkim

Bhattacharya and Chanda (1986) investi¬gated a sub-surface gray peat layer which was detected at Lindok forest near Gangtok, Sikkim at an altitude of 540m. above M.S.L. The pollen analytical results suggest that the late-Quaternary vegetation of Sikkim was locally originated and was quite different from the present day vegetation. The pollen recovered from the sediment were of temperate vegetation type originating from Pinus, Abies, Picea, Alnus, Betula, Acer, Castanopsis, Edgeworthia, etc. along with a large number of ferns.

Meghalaya

Gupta and Sharma (1986) investigated six samples of moss cushion and humus, two each from Shillong peat, Elephanta falls and Mawphlang in Khasi and Jaintia hills of Meghalaya. The results revealed that more than 50% of the total vegetation was similar to the modern forest type in the past samples. The dominant pollen types were Pinus, Quercus, Castanopsis, Ternstroemia, Betula, Taxus, Cinnamomum, Dillenia, etc., depicting temperate vegetation along with some sub-tropical elements.

Western India -Gujarat

Vishnu-Mittre and Sharma (1979) worked on the Holocene deposits (10000 - 5000 yrs. B.P.) from the Nal lake, about 60 km South-West of Ahmedabad suggesting the existence of an open grassland with Chenopod-Savannah type of vegetation. The people of the upper Palaeolithic to Neolithic periods lived in an environment where progressive aridity was recorded.

The different phases of evolution of mangrove vegetation was established through pollen analysis of a two-meter deep profile of Navlakhi, the eastern part of Gulf of Kutch (Caratini et al. 1980). The abundance of Chenopods and stray occurrence of Rhizophoraceae and Avicennia were observed in bottom samples, while Avicennia showed its high frequency in the middle zone and subsequently reduced in the upper zone of the profile. The gradual loss of such mangrove taxa in the South Kutch area may be due to human interference. Ratan and Chandra (1983) analysed 13 surface samples of Gulf of Kutch. The pollen spectra of surface samples showed resemblance with the existing vegetation of the area.

Tamil Nadu and The Nilgiris

Pollen analysis of the samples of Pykara near Ootacamund (Menon, 1967) suggested the dominance of grasses succeeded by fern and other pteridophytic spores, indicating that the early stage was represented by a drier climate gradually changing into a more moist condition. Rao and Menon (1969) reported the presence of fungal remains and epidermal bits referable to grasses from Pykara sediments.

Several surface samples and a 30000 years old profile from Colgrain, Ootacamund of Nilgiris was worked out by Gupta and Prasad (1985). The pollen diagram revealed four climatic phases, namely, warm and humid, more warm and less humid, less warm and more humid, and cool and humid. Pollen analysis were also carried out by Vishnu-Mittre and Gupta (1971) at the Ootacamund region for reconstructing the past vegetation.

Coastal Kerala, Karnataka

Van Campo (1983) investigated bore-core samples, dated to be ca 22000 yrs. B.P., located 10°N offshore Kerala and 15°N offshore Karnataka. Pollen analysis of bottom samples, dated back to 22000 -18000 yrs. B.P., of offshore Kerala Coast has recorded a few mangrove plants depicting dry climatic condition. In successive phase during 11000 yrs. B.P. a good amount of mangrove taxa was recorded representing humid climatic condition. In the last phase, after 6000 yrs. B.P., mangrove taxa began to decline and ultimately disappeared at the top of the core due to biotic influence. Palynological analysis of a 4.25 m deep bore-core sample were studied from Kandavara in Coondapur, about 7 km from Karnataka coast revealed the presence of a mangrove forest Tissot (1990). It was established that the sea level remained unchanged during 6000 yrs. B.P. and the deposition of sediments in the area took place under lagoonal condition.

Karnataka

Pollen analysis of a 1.30m thick profile from Balsudippa of Godavari delta has recorded high values of mangrove vegetation with the presence of dinoflagellates and micro-foraminifera, suggesting the profile's proximity to the sea (Caratini et al. 1980). The presence of Casuarina pollen from bottom to top of the profile suggests the age of the sediment to be around 50 yrs BP. Another 115 cm deep profile from Bairavapalayam of Godavari delta was palynologically analyzed (Caratini et al. 1980). The results revealed high frequency of Chenopodiaceae with low values of mangrove vegetation and scanty presence of dinoflagellates and microforaminifera suggesting that sediment was not under the direct influence of sea.

Two profiles each from southern (Muthupet) and northern (Pichavaram) regions of Caveri delta dated to be ca. 2000 yrs. B.P. were palynologically analysed by Tissot (1987). Analysis of two profiles of Muthupet, 1.50m and 6m thick and about 3 km away from coastline revealed four vegetational periods. Period 'A' showed poor presentation of mangrove plants with clear and constant marine influence. Period 'B' recorded enhanced values of both mangrove and marine elements. Period 'C' revealed maximum growth and development of mangroves with declined marine elements. Period 'D' recorded disappearance of both mangrove and marine elements and eventually succeeded by herbaceous halophytes, possibly due to the geomorphological changes resulting in heavy sedimentation and prograding the delta.

Analysis of pollen content of 51 surface soil samples collected in tropical evergreen and deciduous forests from the western ghats of south India revealed picture of decreased rainfall.(Barboni and Bonnefille.2001).Similar kind of pollen analytical work was undertaken by Anupama et al. (2000) in South India and Sri Lanka to map the vegetation in the study area.

The interpretation of modern pollen rain from the southern Eastern Ghats has been discussed to compare the past vegetation history by pollen sequences and to reconstruct palaeoecological biodiversity. (Anupama,et al., 2000,2002;)

Palaeovegetation studies indicate that about 18,000 and 8,000 years ago, NW India was a moist region; the region could have supported a developing, maritime, riverine civilization, as seen from a study of palaeovegetation maps. There are also indications, from over 1500 archaeological sites located on river

20

banks (Sindhu and Sarasvati), that the Himalayan Rivers were in full flow, for nearly two millennia, around ca. 3300 B.C. The Palaeovegetation studies indicate that the river migrations in NW India and the secular sequence of desiccation of Sarasvati River led to migrations of people, ca. 1500 B.C., from this river basin towards the Ganga-Yamuna doab and south/east of the Gulf of Khambat (Robert, 1993)

Examples of comparative studies in paleoenvironment:

1.ASIA

In the last deglaciation, which is the period of late Pleistocene to early Holocene, have occurred abrupt climatic oscillations. However there are little reports concerned with detailed climatic oscillations during the last deglaciation in East Asia region. Palaeoenvironmental changes in East Asia terrestrial region using the varied lacustrine sediments. The study of Lake Suigestu have preserved detailed and continuous palaeoenvironmental changes for past (kitagawa et al, 2001).

2. Nile floods data and Indian monsoon

It has been established by Palaeovegetation and archaeological studies that there is a close relationship between Indian monsoon rain and Nile floods, for the simple reason that NE Africa gets the same monsoon rain that we have in India. The Nile was flooded because of floods in the Blue Nile in Ethiopia.

The Nile floods data is available for the last five thousand years, the earliest one belonging to circa 2900 BC. The earlier records are rather sporadic but are available for almost every year from 621 AD to 1520 AD. How reliable this data is, becomes clear from extremely low Nile levels during 1396-1408 when there was a devastating famine in India that is well documented and is known as the 'Durgadevi' famine. It is therefore, clear that when Nile was flooded, India had a good monsoon. When the Nile level was low, India had a drought. This is very well collaborated by the epochs of prosperity and decline in Indian history. (Dhavlikar, 2001). Against the backdrop of previous work we prefer to get in to the various details of the study area as illustrated in chapter II.

2

Lacustral Site of Mansar Under Investigation

Survey of the study area:-

The main source for pollen analysis are the sediment samples, from a particular place, sequence and specific depth. Such study require a prerequsit of an extensive study of geomorphology, lithostratigraphy and sediment study of the study area. Field work was conducted for eight seasons (2000-2004) at the Mansar lake and surriounding regions.

The ancient Mansar lake site is located (21020'N 70015'E) at 50 Km. distance North East region of Nagpur district, Taluka – Ramtek The site under investigation for reconstruction of past environment in study area is a dried lake bed near archaeological sites belonging to the Wataka, Sathvahana and Yadav period which are recently being excavated by the Bodhisatva Nagarjuna Smarak and Research Institute,Mansar(Nagpur).It appeared that sediment deposited within this shallow water, artificially created lake is primarily clayey silt with distinct dark brown hue,yet not rich in organic carbon and pollen,but the perennial water body contain sediments with pseudo-vertic characters.This aspect needed detailed multifold investigations.

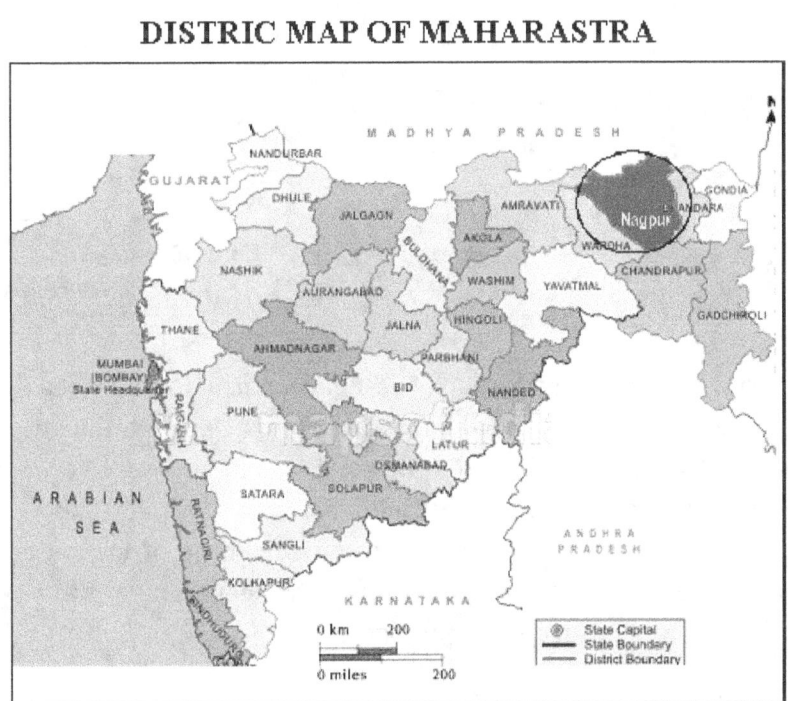

DISTRIC MAP OF MAHARASTRA

In order to understand the exact location and geological features around the Mansar lake , maps and toposheets were referred (No. 550 – katol quarter inch Topo sheets – 50018', 55011', 55015', 5507') published by the Geological Survey of India.

A contour map of the Mansar lake had to be developed, as it was a small region and not covered by the Geological Survey of India. Hence a contour map of the lake site of Mansar was prepared by taking the Ramtek railway station as the main reference point. The methodology implemented for the survey was a physical maping technique using Dumpi level and extensive measurements using measuring tapes by taking into consideration a central reference point of the Mansar lake. Thus an indigenus countour map was developed for making further studies.

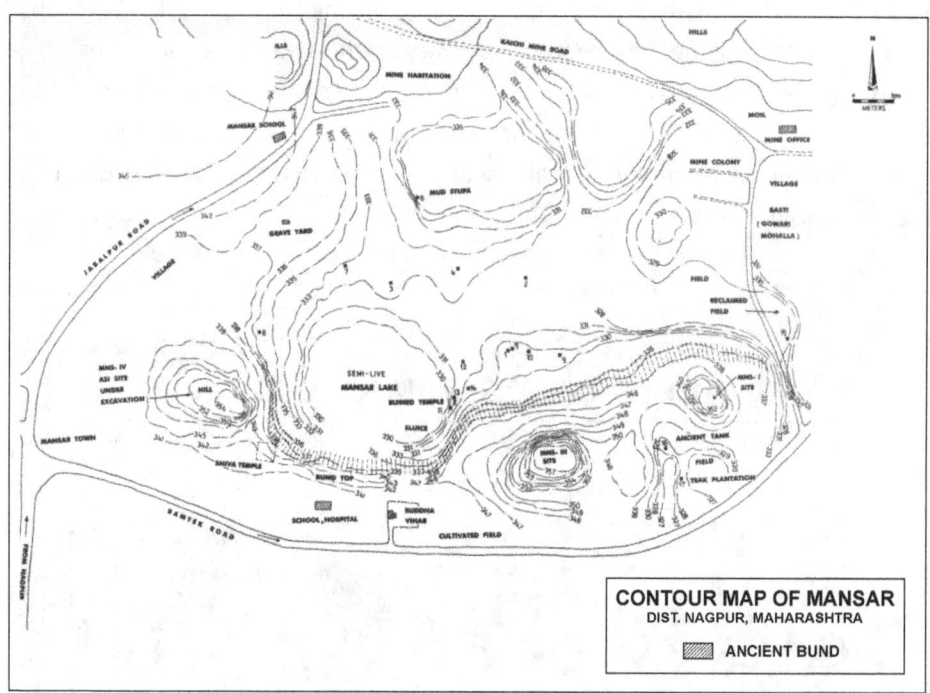

The site for the investigation for reconstruction of past environment in study area in the dried lake bed near archaeological site. Mansar is an autocthonous lake surrounded on three sides (S,N and E) by low Precambrian hillocks,with gneiss- schist and Mn rich schists with abundant vein quartz, quartzite etc. Bunding in Early Historic period (2nd c.B.C.) was laid.,situated at 1000-1200 ' above sea level, with rain fall about 1000-1200 mm per annum. The lake has some drainage of low order from north, north eastern side.The lake have twelve feet water coloumn in the deepest part of the lake in May-June and there is rise in water level by 5 to 6 m during monsoon.

Geographical, Geological and Ecological Settings

Maharashtra state was part of Bombay presidency during the British rule. Its political boundary extends from Bombay to Gadchiroli and Dhule to sindhudurg and Kolhapur district. It is about 800 km East- West and 700 km north – south, lying between 160'4to 2201' N latitude and 72061' to 80091'E longitude having an area of 3,07,690 km.It's limits are Arabian sea on the West whose coast line extends up to 720 km the political states - namely; Goa and Karnataka in the South, Andra Pradesh in the South – East, Madhya Pradesh in the North and Gujarat in the North- west.

The North- Eastern portion of the state comprising basins of Wardha and Vainganga Rivers are known as Nagpur plains. The Wardha basin has the characteristic black soil of the Deccan, but geologically it is in the transition zone. Minerals, especially coal are found in this region. Here the rainfall is heavy, 125 cm. The valley floors and its adjoining hills are thickly forested with bamboo, the soils are lateritic and the geological formation is quite different from those of plateaus. The region has the largest known concentration of the mineral deposit in the state. The early cultivation in India was associated with this region in Maharashtra.

Coal reserves to the tune of 60.97 million tones have been found in Nagpur, Chandrapur and Yavatmal District of the Vidharba region. The black cotton soil is one of the oldest group of soils since the Tertiary era. The temperature and rainfall where the black cotton soils occurs support dry deciduous forests or a thorn savannah. They have 40-60 percent clay contents.

A long and protracted character of volcanic action is evident in many places in Maharashtra in the form of dykes and sills, fossilized water, channels and beheaded rivers like Vaitarna, Umred river etc.

Even after continuous erosion of millions of years the Deccan trap still cover an area of 5,17,998 sq.km. Their abrupt ending along the west coast there they are thickest and form the great scarp of the Western Ghats leaves no real measure of their original extension into the tract of land that foundered in to the Arabian sea.The most significant feature of the Deccan trap are the laterite soils and intertrappean beds containing fossils. Vidarbha belongs to lower traps, lavas with a few ash beds, intertrappean beds, many rich in fossils both plant and animal. (Mahabale and Chaudhari ,1987) .

Climate of Vidarbha

Vidarbha comprises eight districts namely; Buldhana, Yeotmal, Akola, Amravati, Wardha, Nagpur, Bhandara, and Chandrapur. Of these the climate of seven district except Chandrapur is somewhat similar. The northern and western parts of Vidarbha are climatically similar, but the eastern sand southern parts of Bhandara and Chandrapur are rather different. The climate is hot and dry in seven districts mentioned above, as they are in a continuation of Marathwada and Desh part of western Maharashtra.The black cotton soils absorb a lot of heat from sun's radiation during day time in summer months April to June, and emanate it at night. Nagpur in Vidarbha is one of the hottest places in India, the highest temperature being (480C) in eastern Vidarbha at Chandrapur, Bhandara and Nagpur the summer. Pre monsoon showers and thunderstorms in this region are not uncommon. The mean vapour pressure at Nagpur is highest in May. (19-74mm) And lowest in December (4-37 mm). The highest annual rainfall in Vidarbha is 1736 mm. In the region of western Vidarbha the temperature are quite high making the Summers very hot and dry. The annual mean being more than 40 0C. The rainfall is about 975 mm. It also receives some rain due to return monsoons during October and November. The thunderstorms are quite common in this region. In mountainous region and valleys. There are in winter.The eastern part of Vidarbha comprising Chandrapur, Bhandara and Nagpur gets substantial rains from the Bay of Bengal monsoon current in August to September and even later. The humidity becomes high and temperature low. The rainfall is between 1200-1400 mm.

The average annual rainfall in the district is 1161.7 mm it is well distributed increasing from west to east. It is highest in July. 90% of it is received from June to September. On an average, there are 59 rainy days. May is the hottest month when the mean maximum temperature goes to 45 0C , nights are relatively cool and less hot.The thunder storms begin to increase with the beginning of monsoons in the second week of June and the temperature drops down. The minimum temperature in winter can be as low as 4 0C (39 0F). Winds are moderate. November and December are cold months. December is coldest. The soils supports rich forest vegetation. Consequently making Chandrapur and Bhandara districts as the best forested zones of Maharashtra with a lot of biodiversity.

Agroclimatic zones of Vidarbha

There are eight Climatic zones in this region. Our study area comes under zone 8 where there is moderate rainfall. This includes Nagpur district which receives 900 mm of rain on western side and 1250 mm on eastern side. Soils are grey or deep black, trap soils. All kharif (rain feed) and rabi (winter crops) crops grow here especially on heavy soils.

Soils of Vidarbha

Most of the soils in Maharashtra are formed from the Deccan traps generally from the augite or amygdaldial basalt. These soils are black. Dark brown or reddish in colour. Some soils in Nagpur, Bhandara, and Chandrapur district are derived from Vindhyan and Goandwana formations. The Vidarbha soils are formed by the Archaean, the Vindhyans, the Gondwanas and the traps.Vainganga, Purna and Pranahita rivers drain the area. They get both south west as well as north east monsoon rainfall. They therefore support rich monsoon forests in 'Melghat' and 'Chikhaldara' area in Amravati district and 'Allapali forest' in Chandrapur district the Vindhyan soils of Nagpur and Bhandara districts. They have a fair amount of calcium in the form of nodules (kankar) or in layers that reduces the salinity of soils. The structure of this soil is usually cloudy, sometimes crumby with aggregates having natural cleavages. Black soil in general are calcareous, neutral to mild alkaline in reaction. (pH 7.2 – 8.5), high in clay contents.

The most characteristic black soils cap the volcanic plateau of Deccan trap forming a mantle of rich residual soils of moderate depth. There are a few passes with easy gradation to the disintegrated lava (murram) of red to brown colour. There are also alluvial black soils, the profiles of which are much deeper. In general these soils are very fertile except in the uplands where they show low fertility. Calcium and Magnesium carbonates and iron are found in appreciable proportion with variable proportions with variable quantities of potash. These soils are, however, poor in organic matter, Nitrogen and Phosphorus.

An example of soil characteristics of Vidarbha region.

Description	Medium black soil
Location	Trap
Climate	Arid
Rainfall mm	635- 762
Vegetation	Grass, semi humid vegetation
Topography	Undulating
Depth (m)	1-1.5
Texture	Clay – loam
Colour	Greyish black
Nitrogen (mgm)/ 100 gs	40-50
C/N ratio	12 -15
HCl soluble P_2O_5 (mgm / 100gms)	60-100
HCl soluble K_2O (mgm / 100gms)	150-300
Available P_2O_5 (mgm / 100gms)	10-15
Available K_2O (mgm / 100gms)	15-20
Lime ($CaCO_3$)	1-5
Total soluble salt	< 0.2
Base exchange capacity (M.E./ 100 g)	30-60
Base saturation	100
Percentage sodium saturation	<10
$_pH$	7.5-8.5

Climate of Nagpur district

The lake of Mansar is located in the district of Nagpur. Thus is was considered important to have an account of the various climatic factors. The climate of this district is characterised by a hot summer, well distributed rainfall and dryness except in the rainy season. The cold season is from December to February and is followed by the hot season from March to May. The southwest monsoon season is from June to September while the period October-November constitutes the post-monsoon season.

Rainfall:

Records of rainfall in the district are available for 11 stations for periods ranging from 32 to 50 years.(1933 to 2003) The average annual rainfall in the Nagpur district is 1101.4 mm. The rainfall generally increases from the west to the east in the district. The southwest monsoon usually reaches the district in the second week of June. The rainfall during the period June to September constitutes about 87% of the annual total, July being the month with the highest rainfall. The variation in the annual rainfall from year to year is not large. In fifty year period (1941 to 1990), the highest annual rainfall amounted to 144% of the normal for the district occurred in 1944. The lowest annual rainfall in the same fifty year period which was 57% of the normal occurred in 1972. The rainfall was less than 80% of the normal in 8 years out of fifty, of which no years were consecutive. The rainfall in the district as a whole was between 701 and 1400 mm in 45 years out of 50. On an average there are 55 rainy days (i.e. days with rainfall of 2.5 mm or more) in a year.

Temperature:

There are two meteorological observatories in the district, one at Nagpur city and other is at Nagpur Mayo Hospital, records of which are available for a long period of years. The data of these observatories may be taken as representative of the meteorological conditions in the district in general. The cold weather commences towards the end of November and December is usually the coldest month with the mean daily maximum temperature around about 28°C and the mean daily minimum temperature is about 13°C. In the wake of western disturbances which pass across north India in the cold season, the district is sometimes affected by cold waves when the minimum temperature may go down to 4°C. From the beginning of March, temperature begin to rise rapidly.

May is the hottest month with the mean daily maximum temperature is about 42.5°C. The heat during the summer season is severe during the day, the nights being relatively cooler. The afternoon heat is sometimes relieved by thundershowers. The onset of the southwest monsoon by about the second week of June brings welcome relief from the heat, with a considerable drop in temperature. With the withdrawal of the southwest monsoon by about the beginning of October, the day temperature show a slight increase in October and thereafter begins to fall, while the night temperature decrease after September.

The highest maximum temperature ever recorded at Nagpur was 47.8°C on 26th May 1954 and the lowest minimum temperature ever recorded was 3.90C on 7th January 1937. The highest maximum temperature ever recorded at Nagpur (Mayo Hospital) was 47.3°C on 29lh May 1973 and the lowest minimum temperature ever recorded was 7.4°C on 5th January 1991.

Humidity:

Except during the monsoon season when the humidity is high (70-80%) the air is generally dry. The summer season is the driest part of the year when the relative humidity may go down to 20% or less particularly in the afternoons.

Cloudiness:

Skies are mainly heavily clouded to overcast in the southwest monsoon season. In the post monsoon months, moderate cloudiness is common. In the rest of the year the skies are usually clear or lightly clouded. But cloudiness increases on many summer afternoons.

Winds:

Winds are generally light to moderate with some increase in speed in the latter part of the summer season and the monsoon months. During the monsoon season winds are mostly from directions between southwest and northwest. In January winds from directions between north and northeast are common in the mornings and from northeast, east and southeast in the afternoons. While the winds in the mornings in February and March are as in January, the afternoon winds become variable. In the rest of the summer season winds are mostly from directions between west and northwest. In the period from October to December the winds are mainly northerly to northwesterly in the mornings and northeasterly to easterly in the afternoons.

Special weather phenomena:

In the monsoon months, depressions from the Bay of Bengal move westwards across the central parts of the country and affect the district and its neighbourhood causing widespread heavy rain and strong winds. Thunderstorms occur in all seasons although their frequency is very small in the period November to January and maximum in monsoon months with average frequency about 10 days in a month. The frequency of squall is more in summer months, being maximum.(i.e. 4 to 6). Occasional fog is noticed from August to February. (Meteorology Department, Govt.of India- 2003). In order to understand the floristic composition in the study area, the reserve forest patches in Chandrapur district were explored since these are the only reserve area where maximum forest cover is seen in Maharashrta. The following information on Chandrapur region are documented so as to understand the contemporary forest dynamics and for getting insight into the palaeovegetational dataset.

The climate of Chandrapur district

The climate of this district is characterised by hot summer, well distributed rainfall the southwest monsoon and general dryness except in the rainy season. The cold season extended from December to February. This is followed by the hot season, from March to May. The southwest monsoon season is from June to September. October and November constitute the post-monsoon season.

Rainfall:

The rainfall in the district generally increases from the west towards the east and varies from 1151.4 mm at Warora to 1442.8 and 1448.4 mm. The rainfall during southwest monsoon season from June to September constitutes about 89% of the annual rainfall. July is the rainiest month. The variation in the rainfall from year to year is large. During the fifty-year period (1941 to 1990) the highest annual rainfall in the district was 165% as compared to the records of 1959 to 1972.where the lowest annual rainfall which was only 58 % . On an average, there are 58 rainy days in a year in the district.

Temperature:

The mean daily maximum temperature in May is about 420C to 430C and the mean daily minimum is about 27 to 28°C. The heat in summer is intense during the day, especially in the southern parts of the district. Occasionally the day temperature rise upto 48°C The afternoon heat is sometimes relieved by thundershowers. With the onset of southwest monsoon in the district by about the middle of June the temperature decrease appreciably. During early October while southwest monsoon withdraws from the district the day temperature increase a little and a secondary maximum is reached in October. Later, both day and night temperature decrease progressively. The decrease in night temperature is rapid. The maximum temperature ever recorded at Brahmapuri was 47.7°C and the lowest minimum temperature ever recorded was 4.6°C.

In the month of October, both day and night temperatures decrease progressively till December which is the coldest month. In the northern parts of the district, the mean daily maximum temperature in December is 28.0°C and the mean daily minimum temperature is 12.80C. The mean daily maximum temperature in the southern half of the district is 28.9°C and the mean daily minimum is 12.80C. During the winter season, cold season, cold spells affect the district in association with the passage of western disturbances across north India. The minimum temperature on such occasions may go down to about 3°C. Temperature rise rapidly after February till May which is the hottest month of the year.

Humidity:

The air is generally dry over the district except during the southwest monsoon season when the humidity is about 70-80%. The summer months are the driest when the relative humidity in the afternoons varies between 20 and 25%.

Cloudiness and Winds:

The skies are heavily clouded to overcast during the southwest monsoon season. In the rest of the year, skies are lightly clouded.Winds are generally light with some increase in the wind force during the latter the summer season and in the southwest monsoon season. In the post-monsoon and cold seasons winds blow mostly from directions between north and northeast. In the first half of the summer season winds gradually change over to direction between east and south-east in the mornings and north-northwest in the afternoons and by May winds from direction: between south and northwest become more common. During the southwest monsoon season the winds are mainly from the directions between south or west.

Special weather phenomena:

Thunderstorms occur in all the months, their incidence being highest during the summer and monsoon season and the lowest during the cold season. Occasional dust storms occur during the summer months. Fog sometimes occur in the post monsoon and cold seasons.

During the monsoon depressions that originate in the Bay of Bengal, the air move westwards and the district experiences strong winds and widespread heavy rain. Less frequently, storms and depressions from the Bay of Bengal during the post-monsoon also affect the weather.

Archaeological background: Mansar lake site.

The Mansar site has a special significance in the early history of Maharashtra as it was the capital of the Vakataka rulers (c. 3rd to 7th Century A.D.) However the history of the site goes back to 1st to 5th Century B.C. as evidenced by the recent archaeological excavations at Hidimba Tekdi carried out by the Archaeological survey of India.It is a temple complex site on schist- quartzite steeply dipping hillock close to the fresh water perennial lake. According to Dr.Sharma the antiquity of the lake goes back to 2nd B.C. Terracotta objects of Satavahana, Vakataka, Maurya and Shunga period have been reported from the site.

However, the site was also reported much earlier by Wellsted (1934) He has mentioned a 'burial shaft' that existed between Ramgiri and Hidimba Tekdi. The brick structural complex found is suggested to be the sanctum centre of a temple structure (Pravaresvardevakulasthana) mentioned in the Vakataka inscription of the King Pravarsena II (395 to 419 A.D.). On the basis of the evidence of a factory site, a religious seals found indicates that the place was a religious capital of the Vakatakas. The seals have Brahmi script an inscription reading 'Pravaresvaray'; justifying the name Pravaresvardevakulasthana.

Other such inscriptions exist at the Narsimha temple at Ramtek near Mansar. However all scholars do not yet conclusively accept the suggestion of Manasar being the religious capital of the Vakatakas. Apart from this, the site of Mansar has yielded remains of various religious complexes including three Buddhist stupas, two chaityas and sixteen shrines. The shrines are built in the shape of a lotus. Six shivlingas were also found. During the excavations conducted by us at MNS-XIV,a mixed artefactual assemblage was found that includes pottery, terracotta beads, brickbats and also microlithic blades. However, this assemblage was collected from the lake deposits of the Mansar lake it was not possible to pinpoint their stratigraphic and hence chronological context. Some microlithic blades were also collected from the Pleistocene terrace in the vicinity.

Modern vegetation study-Nagpur-Chandrapur Region

Forest divisions and ranges in Vidarbha:

The forest area in Maharashtra state is 63,798 sq.km. The total geographical area of the state is 3,07,690 sq.km out which the forest area is 15%. the total forest cover is 46,143 sq.km .Out of which 23622 sq.km. is dense forest, 22,397 sq.km is open forest and 124 sq.km. is mangrove forests.

The are eleven forest circles, 43 divisions and five subdivisions. The following table gives forest circles, divisions and the forest area of Vidarbha region.

Name of circle	Division	No. of ranges	Forest area sq.km.
Nagpur	• Nagpur • Wardha • Bhandara • Gondia	31	8293
North Chandrapur circle	• Brahmapuri • Wadsa • Chandrapur • Gadchiroli	17	7676
South Chandrapur circle	• Allapalli • Bhamragad • Sironcha • Central Chandrapur	24	11,100

Forest of Vidarbha

The flora of Maharashtra is heterogenous in composition. As regards the general flora, there are many species in the flora of Vidarbha, which are different from those in remaining Maharashtra, There are many different herbs and climbers. Here shrubs are common Gnetum ula, Carvia callosa are uncommon. In the flora of western Maharashtra there are endemic or very rare species, but in the flora of Vidarbha such endemic species hardly a few, have been recorded. It is the only area where teak or Tectona grandis is self-sown. The vigorous growth of Tectona grandis and other woody species as found in Vidarbha is not seen in other parts of Maharashtra.

A perusal of the list of plants in Nagpur, Tadoba, Pench valley, Ramtek, Pipperhetty and Kolsa areas clearly shows that there are large number of herbaceous species here. The shrubs are rather sparse in the flora of Vidarbha. The trap hills around Nagpur and Tadoba are covered in monsoon by herbaceous ephemeral ground flora.

31

Flora of Vidarbha

Vidarbha stands on an upland plateau having nearly 457- 549 m elevation above M.S.L. It is a continuous stench of land with black cotton soils derived from the Deccan Trap basalt. The major rivers of this region are Wardha, Penganga, Katepurna, and Purna. The climate of Vidarbha is hot and dry. The comprehensive flora of Maharashtra as such has not been compiled earlier although distinct floras are available. The most important work available so for dealing with flora of Maharashtra was Cooke's "Flora of presidency of Bombay (1901- 1908) .A major lacuna in Cooke's flora is that flora of Vidarbha had not been included. Mahable and Chaudhari(1987) has published the Botany and flora of Maharashtra as an invaluable reference book. Mirashi (1954) and his team from Nagpur University have published many papers on Asteraceae, Cyperaceae, Tubiflorae,List of hydrophytes from Nagpur and new records of Nagpur district as precusrsors to the Flora of Nagpur. Ugemuge (1986) has published a book on flora of Nagpur district. Recently many district floras have been worked out by the Botanical Survey of India, Pune, such as Flora of Maharashtra.(1996, 2000, 2001)

Flora of Akola has been published(Kamble and Pradhan, 1988).A list of hydrophytes from Nagpur area was published by Mirashi.(1954).Flora of "Tadoba National Park (Chandrapur) has been published comprising 667 species by Malhotra and Moorthy in 1992.

A few lists of plants in different parts of Vidarbha are available. As early as 1887, here Van Somaran had published "A list of trees in Melghat forest" giving account of 110 trees in the Melghat forest" followed by " A list of trees shrubs and climbers in the northern circle of central provinces." A descriptive list of trees, shrubs and economic herbs of Southern circle of the central provinces have been made by Graham (1911) particularly of Nagpur plants, about 309 species.

Balapure (1966)a has prepared list of Nag- Vidarba, Ramtek flora. He has estimated about 2000 plants in old central province. Malhotra and Moorthy (1971,1992) have described 500 species in Chandrapur District. It is obvious that the flora here is very rich containing dry deciduous, semi- evergreen and some moist evergreen species. The well-known tiger and wild game Reserve Tadoba sanctuary lies, in the explored region. A general survey for floristic analysis and collection of comparative pollniferous materials was undertaken.

The forest divisions in Vidarbha region are as followes;

North Circle: Five Divisions namely,

1) Tadoba

2) Brahmapuri

3) Chandrapur

4) Wadsa

5) Gadchiroli

South circle:Six Divisions namely,

1) Chandrapur
2) Allapalli
3) Ballarshaha
4) Sironcha
5) Bhamaraghar
6) Chaprala

The Tectona grandis and other timber species grow very luxuriantly here and yield highest revenue to the state. On the whole the vegetation in Vidarba is the dry mixed deciduous type in which Tectona predominates. The Vegetation however changes and assumes different facies according to location, topography, soils, altitude, rainfall, humidity etc. in different months of the year.

A comprehensive list of plants is given here (ref Appendix). The floristic survey was carried out, following consecutive seasons to explore the flora in Monsoon, winter and summer season. The plants are collected, in various seasons, and herbarium sheets are prepared. The plants are collected form Nagpur, Ramtek, Tadoba, Kolsa, Pipperhetty, pench area. The plants are photographed in flowering state. Total number of plants comprising 97 families, 369 Genera and 500 Species. have been collected and enlisted. The plants of Nagpur, Ramtek and around are like those of many other semi-humid or sub-humid places of Maharashtra. However because of high rainfall and undulating topography there are many lakes in this region, some permanent.

The vegetation is dry deciduous with occasional patches of moist deciduous species. Tectona grandis plantation is found in almost all districts. Anogeissus latifolia and Haldina cordifolia occur throughout in region . In chandrapur, Gadchiroli, vegetation is rich, and the growth of teak is luxuriant. A variety of cereals-Hordeum vulgare, oryza sativa, setaria italica, Pulses- cajanus cajan, Lablab purpureus, Pisum sativum, vigna spp, Oil seeds- Arachis hypogea, Brassica spp, Sesamum orientale and vegetables, condiments, Narcotics- Nicotiana tobaccum, many fruits, and Saccharrum officinarum are cultivated.

According to Champion (1936), the forests of this region can be classified into two main types

1)Moist tropical forests (South Indian deciduous forests)

2) Dry troical forest.

Dry tropical forest is common in study area.

It can be subdividied into two types. i) Scrub forest ii) Southern tropical dry deciduous forests.

The Southern Tropical Dry Deciduous forest is further divided into

a)   Dry teak bearing forest and

b)   Southern Dry Mixed Deciduous forests: - There is concentration of thorny species in this type. Availability of grasses and plants useful as fodder is plentiful. This forest types occurs in Bhandara, Chandrapur, Gadchiroli, Nagpur and Yavatmal.

A comphrensive list of common trees, shrubs, climbers and herbs are documented from this region.

The identification of plants with latest names and authorites have been done according to the latest floras.(Singh et al,2001;Sharma et al 1996; Singh and Karthikeyan 2000; Yadav and Sardesai,2002) The closely related families are illustrated as per Benthem and Hooker's system of plant classification.

The dominant families of flowering plants are herewith stated in order of dominance from the study area;

1)   Poaceae
2)   Fabaceae
3)   Cyperaceae
4)   Acanthaceae
5)   Asteraceae
6)   Rubiaceae
7)   Euphorbiaceae
8)   Lamiaceae
9)   Combretaceae
10)   Mimosae
11)   Verbenaceae
12)   Scrophulariaceae
13)   Rutaceae
14)   Tiliaceae
15)   Convolvulaceae
16)   Orchidaceae

3

The Palynological Approach

METHODOLOGY

Pollens analysis was conducted from Trenches MNS –I, II, III, IV, V, VI, IX, X and XIV . Where MNS, XIV has been considered as a central reference trench so as to understand the palynological lake history of Mansar. In order to study these samples various strategies were implemented ranging from the importance of pollen analysis to sediment analysis from various stratigraphic sequences of the profiles exposed in the trenches.

Resons for using pollen and spores as indicators of past climate :

1) Due to the presence of resistant chemical sporopollenin in exine pollen and spores are considerably preserved in deposits .

2) Pollen and spores are very small in size, dispersed to as certain distance from their source. Thus they represent a flora from a wider area of surrounding land.

3) Pollen and spores show a great morphological diversity that help even up to species level of identification.

4) Pollen and spores are produced in huge quantities. So a small portion of sediment is enough to get considerable amount of pollen grains.

Pollens show the great morphological diversity of pollen and spores characteristics of living plants, which is of taxonomic importance. Since the pollen grain exine is resistant ,it may have a long geological life.It gets incorporated into sediments. Studies of the morphological hangs of spores during subsequent ages make possible to understand their evolutionary development and the plants associated with them. Because of the wide dispersal of spores in sediments, this approach to evolutionary analysis promises to be rewarding.(Nair,1962).

Deposits analysed for fossil pollen and spores from Mansar Lake

The principle fresh water environments., where pollen grains are now being deposited and preserved in the Mansar lake are rather shallow and perennial . The lake It is made up of autochthonous (in – situ) and allochthonous materials. It contains large proportion of allochthonous material derived from the plants outside the lake basin. It consists of inorganic and organic materials of local vegetation and an input of local pollen direct from the air via drainage water. According to the nutrient status the sediment in the beginning was from entrophic lake type, where nutrient availability is high, leading to high productivity. The sediment contains large proportion of organic material and mud. Algae, aquatic plants are producer organisms. It is highly calcareous deposit.

Lake Sediments:

The lake sediments are good source of pollen and spores. Works have been done on the different strata of soil profile. It is evident that soil having pH less that 5 contain considerable quantities of pollen, up to half a million per gram (Ertdman, 1969) or 1.5 million per gram of dry soil (Dimbleby , 1957). Soil above a pH level of 6, generally devoid of pollen grains. Good quantities of pollen grains are also recovered from surface and subsurface soil sediments. (Bhattacharya et al 2006; Anupama et al. 2002; Barboni et al. 2001). So the analysis of soils has revealed a distinct stratification of pollen assemblages. Test pit - (MNS-I)Trench- The trench MNS-I was dug as a test pit in dried SE part of the lake Mansar and reached to a depth of about 2.10 m.The sediment at 10 cm depth (Lithounit I) were dark brown vertic with occasional molluscan shells including planorhls and with good proportion of Iron – Manganese soft pellets. In upper 30 cm prismatic peds were well developed and lamination was totally absent, though shells were found to be concentrated at a depth of 15 cm from the surface.

Lower layers (Lithounit II) showed crude lamination, yet strongly disturbed by pedal crumb, slicken surface etc.Pellet size increased to 1 cm in lower layers and they were found to develop at the junction point of two desiccation cracks .These lacustral vertic soil sediments were likely to contain mere organic matter (>1%-1.5 %) than in normal black soil or vertisol developed in- situ ,as a erosion or monophase soil. These sediments were not affected by bio-turbation to any great extent. Occurrence of distinctly bioturbated ferruginous lacustral clay layer at a depth of 110-120 cm or even below suggested temporary drying of the lake sometime after 7th c. B.C. ,as we could observed broken brick bats along with pebble-cobble size stones of Vein quartz and Manganese oxide. Drying of lake was suggested by limonitisation , increase proportion of shells, brick bats, local stones etc. and also by better pedality as seen in litho unit I-II.Discovery of a left lower jaw of a wild bore(Sas serefa Linn.-Wild bore, move in group of 15-20) at a depth of 125 cm within an area of 60-70 sq .cm .show that low energy of lake could not disturb the jaw and canine tooth in small sandy bed.

Layers III (Lithounit III) were relatively free from molluscan shells and Fe-Mn pellets less in number. Bedding was crude yet better preserved than in Litho units I and II.

Layer IV (Lithounit IV) was bioturbated ferruginous clayey layer (1.20 m) gradually graded to sandy clay to clayey sand to ultimately colluvial gravelly clayey sand with chips and blocks of (5-6 cm across),locally derived vein quartz ,granite gneiss, manganese oxide nodules .Gravelly sandy clay suggested occasional sheet floods in the area, yet the lake survived as a very shallow water body ,and surface expression of the deeper lake which probably continued on western side.The Manganese precipitation and degree of ferruginisation increases as the lake got shallower.

Thus apparently change in lake hydrology in last 1000 yrs was obvious. The 14C date have supported this preliminary observations.On northern side there was an excellent preservation of pseudo alluvial fan, partially calcretized (with nodular calcrete) .Good number of microliths were collected. from the surface of this alluvial fan. This fan got dissected prior to the construction of the lake around 2200 yrs. B.P. The MNS-I trench was in the lacustral surface inset into the alluvial fan of the late Pleistocene period.

In recent times the Mansar lake has become oligotrophic, with low nutrient availability therefore, less productive, which contain less organic matter i.e. largely minerogenic, the rate of accumulation is slow and depends on the rate of erosion.

By digging trenches in this series of sediments ,we could obtain a vertical sequence of samples of sediment ,each of which have been deposited at a particular time. Such samples were analyzed for palynomorphs occurrence. With each grain or spore being identified under high power of compound microscope. A pollen diagram was constructed for showing the representation of each taxon identified and its variation with the passage of time . The following steps were considered while collecting the pollen samples:,

- Collection of soil samples

- Pollen analysis and identification

- Production of pollen spectrum

- The vegetation and floristic significance .

- The physical environment from which the sample was drawn.

- The changes in the total environment over a period of time .

- Two aspects are considered in analysis of pollen samples. & present day vegetation in the proposed area.

A) Pollen analysis - Processing the samples by standard methods.

B) Investigating factors determining the relation between vegetation

and pollen present.

POLLEN MORPHOLOGY & PALYNOTAXONOMY

Pollen grains were extracted from various stratigraphic sequences from the study area. Various laboratory protocols were implemented so as to generate a potential database of pollen types. In order to understand the pollen morphology of various species during microscopic observations, it was important to understand the description , shapes, size and sculpturing types of pollen grains.

Shape of pollen grains (polar view) (after Erdtman 1956)

A) **Non – angular** Circular

Elliptic

a) Acuminate

Acute   Obtuse

b) Emarginate

c) Truncate.

B) Angular

b) Quadrangular

Concave   Straight   Convex

c) Quinquangular

Concave   Straight   Convex

38

Shape classes (after Erdtman 1956)

Peroblate

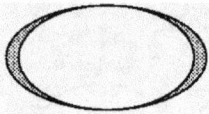

Oblate

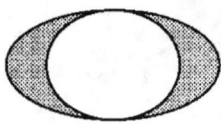

Suboblate

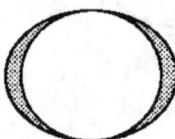

Oblate spheroidal

Spheroidal

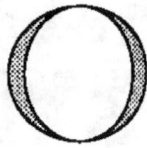

Prolate spheroidal

Subprolate

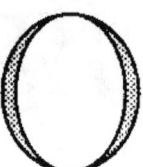

Prolate

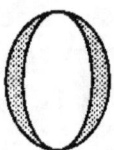

Per-prolate

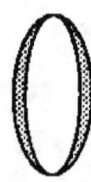

39

NPC classification of pollen (after Erdtman 1969)

ATREME	NOMOTREME							ANOMOTREME
No	N1	N2	N3	N4	N5	N6	N7	N8
	MONO	DI	TRI	TETRA	PENTA	HEXA	POLY	

P0	P1	P2	P3	P4	P5	P6
?	CATA	ANACATA	ANA	ZONO	DIZONO	PANTO

C0	C1	C2	C3	C4	C5	C6
?						
TREME	LEPT	TRICHO TOMO COLPATE	COLPATE	PORATE	COLP ORATE	POR ORATE

Pollen size classes (After Erdtman 1945)

Sr. No.	Pollen size class	Length of longest axis.
1)	Very small grains (sporae perminutae)	< 10 μm
2)	Small grains (Minutae)	10-25 μm
3)	Medium sized grain (Mediae)	25-50 μm
4)	Large grains (Magnae)	50-100 μm
5)	Very large grains (Permagnae)	100-200 μm
6)	Gigantic grains (Giganteae)	> 200 μm

Sculpturing types visible in surface view (After Erdtman 1947)

Surface pattern   **Sculpturing type**

Surface pattern	Sculpturing type	Surface pattern	Sculpturing type
	Psilate		Faveolate
	Echinate		Rugulate
	Granulate		Fossulate
	Rugulate		Striatio reticulate
	Striate		
	Reticulate		Refipilate
	Verrucate		Negative reticulum

Sediment Sampling At Mansar Lake Site

Methodology:

Considerable multidisciplinary research involving mapping of Quaternary formation, locating and excavating archaeological sites for the construction of geological and archaeological sequence, laboratory analysis of sediments, radiometric dating of geological deposits and collection of ethnographic data on agricultural populations was carried out in the study area.

1)   Survey of the study area :-

The main source of pollen analysis are the sediment samples, from a particular place in ,a particular sequence, and at a particular depth. The above requirement needed an extensive study of Geomorphology, lithostratigraphy and sediment study of the study area.

Field work was conducted for eight seasons (2000-2004) at Mansar. Palynolithological sampling and environmental field training was undertaken at few sites.

The study area

Dist – Nagpur

Tal – Ramtek

Village – Mansar

Site – Bodhisatva Nagarjuna & Smarak, and ASI excavation site – Mansar

Location – N.E., Nagpur – 21020'N 70015'E, 50 km N.E. from Nagpur.

The site for the investigation, for reconstruction of past environment in study area is the dried lakebed near archaeological site.

2. Map- Work :

Following maps and toposheets were studied for the exact location of the study area.

1)   No. 55-0 – katol (quarter inch).

2)   Topographic sheets – 50018', 55011', 55015', 5507'

The exact location of the site :

SITE	DESCRIPTION	SHEET NO.	GRID REF	LAT	LONG
Nagpur	Town	55-O	LO96	$21^0 05'$	$79^0 05'$
Mansar	Village	55-O	LP19	$21^0 20'$	$70^0 15'$

The contour map(Fig 3.6 and PWD map of the lake site of Mansar was prepared by taking the Ramtek railway station as the main reference point.

The Approach for sampling:

The fieldwork was focused on the lake site of Mansar encompassing area of 59.69 hectare. In total 22 trenches were dug in and around the Mansar lake area by my guide and I actively participated in the excavations. Sampling was carried out with fresh trench profile method and one complete soil profile was taken to ensure enough recovery of material for both pollen analysis and dating. The sample of 14C dating was collected without any contamination in form of sub fossil shell sample. At the same time few samples were taken for AMS dating and attempts will be made to get them dated in future.

Physico- chemical parameter:

The soil samples collected were analyzed for following physico- chemical parameter.

1)   PH of soil sample.

2)   Determination of organic carbon in soil by colorimetric method., by using methods outlined by Datta et. al. (1962).

3)   Calculation of percent $CaCO_3$

4)   Observation of soil colours from Munshell soil colour chart .

5)   Total phosphorus content in soil sample.

6)   Total fluorine content in soil sample.(Kshirsagar,1990)

Preliminary soil sample analysis:

Soil samples were collected carefully without contamination for pollen analysis. Preliminary pollen analysis of 28 soil samples was undertaken by standard method of Faegri and Iversen (1975) to check the palynomorph potential. Though this method is standard it has been modified in Indian context, where environment is more oxidizing, which prevent preservation of palynomorphs in sediment. The method is already calibrated and standardized by Kajale and Deotare.(1995) ,which is more suitable for the minerogenic and alkaline sediments in high temperature, in Vidarbha region. The preliminary soil sample analysis was undertaken for particle size analysis (Day, 1965;Piper 1966), The chemical analysis of soil sample was carried out to detect carbonates, phosphates, organic carbon, percentage fluorine analysis (Jakson ,1962) ,pH and soil colour (Munshell soil colour chart).

Field Techniques

Uncontaminated samples were collected from the exposed stratigraphic sections in the semi-arid lakebeds and also on the periphery of lake. The following criteria taken in to consideration for the choice of Mansar Lake as a sampling site.

1)   The dried and semi-dried areas of lake deposits were preferred.

2)   As the lake area was about 59.69 hectare in area it was of ideal magnitude for such extensive palaeoecological excavation work.

3)   The samples were collected from the locations which were free from wind or water current during the excavation.

4)   Tributary of Pench river that entered the lake basin, was avoided thus avoiding the risk of contamination, oxidation.

5)   Subsurface and surface samples are collected from the spots, which were free from severe erosion.

Research considerations:

Systematic excavations were carried out at Mansar to understand following aspects of the problem undertaken for study.

1)   To understand lake formation.

2)   To understand changing hydrology of the lake.

3)   To check the original historical boundary of the Man made bund of Mansar Lake.

4) To check the depth of water column and height of the deposits on the Pleistocene terrace and   rate of sedimentation.

5) To find out the possible relevance and correlation of pollen analytical and palaeoenvironmental work with the archaeological site on the top of the hill.

6) Collection of sediment sample for microfossils analysis.

7) To study the lithostratigraphical sequence in the dried lakebeds.

8) To estimate the age of profiles by 14 C dating method.

9) To appreciate the soil Chemistry and its physical properties, and its relation to pollen spore preservation.

10) To conduct mineral magnetic study to understand pedological weathering changes and its palaeoclimatic correlation, if any.

Lithostratigraphical characteristics : trench (MNS-XIV) for stratigraphic differentiation

Taking into consideration the stratigraphic profiles of 22 trenches a generic lithostratigraphic sequence was reconstructed as a composite stratigraphy, which were divided into five-litho unit based on various botanical and geological parameters. In general the trenches show following sediment deposition. Trench MNS- XIV has been selected for detailed study.

LITHOUNIT I-   Uppermost layer 0-40 cm- upper most Black soil (20 cm) with grass cover, vertical cracks observed, Full of modern and sub modern gastropod shells, rootlets, brick bats, pot shreds, beads, etc were observed.

LITHOUNIT II- 40-60 cm- grayish brown clayey silt Well developed blocky peds, iron rhizoconcretions at 45cm in MNS –14. The sediment was compact, organic clay. Rootlets still persist. Gastropods were very small and less in number.

LITHOUNIT III- 60-130 cm- Dark brown, Homogenous, compact, with slicken slit, thick black sticky clay. Shells absent. At the depth of 110 cm $CaCO_3$ coated Manganese pellets were observed.

LITHOUNIT IV- 130-180 cm-Well sorted yellowish brown, sandy mud with occasional MnO_2 concretions is predominant. Occasional gravel, and grayish clay lenses, lots of Manganese nodules were observed. Almost devoid of any organic matter shells absent.

LITHOUNIT V - 180-210 cm- yellowish brown gravelly sand with Manganese Oxide, Iron concretions, Granite gneiss, Mica schist, Vein quartz, Aplite, and occasional large lithoclasts were observed. Shells absent. Microliths were collected. (MNS-II at 135-16 cm)

Sampling procedures:

Grab sampling:

When a suitable spot was selected from the trench, excavated systematically, wall of soil profile was cleaned with a knife and tape is stretched to record the length of the each litho unit of profile. The samples were collected from the bottom to the top of the profile. Each sample after collection was properly labeled indicating the depth range and necessary information and finally packed in zip lock polythene bags and sealed. The lithologs were taken from each section and field numbers of the samples are noted for future reference.

MNS-XIV -TRENCH- STRATIGRAPHIC SAMPLING:

The stratigraphic sections were initially scrapped and marked with labels so as to differentiate the layers. Before undertaking sampling, sections were described and physical features were noted. Each point of grab (undisturbed inner core) samples was noted by using a measuring tape in which the zero marking was always placed at the beginning of horizon 'A'. The grab samples of about 30-40 grams each were scooped out from bottom to top of the profile so as to avoid inter-sample contamination. The samples were collected either in a plastic bag or a container and property labeled, sealed and packed on the site itself. After each sampling the knife/ scoop was washed with distilled water so as to prevent inter sample contamination. After adequate sampling the sections were photographically recorded.

Laboratory Techniques

Laboratory- Glasswares, equipments and Chemicals.

Glass wares – Teflon beakers, Teflon centrifuge tubes, Teflon rods, coffee filters (200 microns) whatman filter paper no. I, Borosil glass coloumns with topper, (1000ml capacity) glass breakers – 2000 ml capacity, Brass filter – 72 micron mesh size, 150 micron mesh size capacity, petridish, suction. Instruments – vacuum operated pump, ultrasonic filter, digital balance. Centrifuge machine, distill water unit, oven, heater, hot water bath, wooden hood with exhaust fan.

Distilled water

Chemicals – HCl – 10%

Sodium hexametaphosphate – 5%

HF – 60%

Acetic anhydride

Conc.H_2SO_4

Glacial acetic acid

KOH-10%

Glycerin-50%

Phenol Crystals

Precaution:

1)   While performing all this procedure, particularly while using KOH, HF one must wear glasses to protect the eyes from the fumes.

2)   All the operations are to be carried out in a wooden hood, equipped with powerful exhaust fan.

Pollen analysis

The samples were analyzed using the standard techniques as suggested by Faegri and Iversen (1964,1975) and with slight modification depending on the sample type. (Deotare 1995) . Here few techniques like use of sodium hexameta phosphate and use of tall glass columns to remove tenacious clay were implemented as suggested by Anupama Krishnamurty (IFP, Pondicherry- personal communication). To improve the recovery of palynomorphs from the tenacious clay and highly minerogenic sediment of Mansar, various methods of sediment analysis were implemented as per the nature of the samples. (Lentfer and Boyd. 1997, 2000,; Jemmett and Owen ,1996; Hunt ,1955).

Pollen / spore extraction procedure

Step- I

Removal of tenacious clay from the sediment:

1. Take 5 gm sample in Teflon beaker- crush the sample in 15 ml of DW.
2. Add 10 % HCl for one hour- transfer the sample in 15 ml TT-
3. Centrifuge at 2000 rpm for 3-5 min- Decant
4. Homogenize in DW and filter through coffee filter of 200μ -transfer the filtrate in 2000 ml beaker and Keep the residue for observation
5. Fill the 2000 ml beaker full to its capacity, cover it with lid and keep it undisturbed for 5-6 hrs.
6. After 5-6 hrs pour off half the quantity of supernatant water and again keep it overnight. - Next day pour the content in to 1 lit glass column.
7. Add 10 ml of 5 % sodium hexametaphosphate,in each column.
8. Keep the column undisturbed overnight- Next day pour off half the quantity of supernatant – shake the content by horizontal panning
9. Add 10 ml of 5 % sodium hexametaphosphate-Mix it by horizontal shaking-Keep undisturbed overnight-
10. Next day if the supernatant is not clear, pour off half of the supernatant by using suction pump.
11. Again add 10 ml Na hexametaphosphate -Make the final volume 1000 ml by adding DW

12. Keep it overnight-Next day if the supernatant is turbid, repeat he procedure ,till the supernatant become clear.

Step II-

HF treatment

1.   Decant off 600 ml of supernatant and keep 400 ml in the column.

2.   Centrifuge it at 2000 rpm for 5 min.- centrifuges all the content of column.

3.   Add 10 % HCl to the residue and Keep the content in HCl for 20 min

4.   Centrifuge- Add 60 % HF, Disperse the content, and pour it in Teflon beaker

5.   Cover the beaker with brown paper and rubber band

6.   Keep the sample in HF for 24 hrs, stirring it after every 12 hr-Decant the HF from beaker

7.   Add 200 ml of 20 % hot HCl in all the beakers and Keep it for 3-4 hrs then Pour off the supernatant of 20 % HCl

8.   Add DW to the beaker full of its capacity – Mix the residue –Keep the beaker overnight- Next day centrifuge the content of the beaker at 2000 rpm- Wash with DW-

9.   Centrifuge at 2000 rpm for 5 min - Give second wash of DW-Centrifuge – decant-Give third wash of DW-centrifuge- Decant-Repeat the procedure till the supernatant become clear.

Step III-

Acetolysis

1.   Take the residue in 10 ml glass TT- Add DW- Centrifuge at 2000 rpm for 3 min.

2.   Decant the supernatant- Repeat Acetolysis Add Glacial acetic acid. Centrifuge- decant-Add Acetolysis mixture (Acetic anhydride: Conc. H2SO4 in 9:1 proportion)

3.   Keep the TT in water bath at 80-85 0C for 5 min-Stir it well. –

4.   Centrifuge at 2000 rpm for 3 min.

5.   Decant the supernatant- Add GAA-Mix it well. Centrifuge-

6.   Decant –Give wash of DW for 2-3 times.

Step IV-

KOH treatment

1.   After wash of DW after Acetolysis add 10 % KOH in the residue.

2.   Disperse the residue in TT- Keep the TT in Hot water bath at 80-85 oC for 5 min.

3.   Transfer the content in a glass beaker of 50 ml capacity.

4.   Sieve the content through 150 -µ mesh- Wash the TT with DW.

5.   Wash the mesh under running tap water.

6.   Centrifuge the content of the beaker in glass TT only.

7.   Wash the residue with DW- Centrifuge. And repeat the washing till the supernatant become clear.

8.   Give final wash of DW –Centrifuge.

9.   Decant DW-Add Small amount of 50 % glycerin.

10.   Store the residue in small vials.

Preparation of permanent reference slides- modern pollen grains

Preparation of glycerin jelly:

Gelatin 50 gm, Glycerin 150 ml, distilled water 175 ml, Phenol crystals 7 gm are the requisite for the preparation of the jelly. The first three constituents are mixed thoroughly and boiled in a water bath for one to two hours. The phenol crystals should be added and mixed thoroughly while still warm and molten, the glycerin jelly should be poured on a petridish making a thin uniform layer of about 0.5 cm thick. It is then cooled and preserved in refrigerator.

Mounting of digested sample and Preparation of slides

A minute piece of glycerin jelly was taken on a clean platinum needle, sterilizing it after each treatment by burning it over a flame. The platinum needle was touched carefully to the bottom of the centrifuge tube where the pollen / spores are precipitated and transfer on a clean slide. Then the slide was heated gently and after the jelly spread evenly by the needle. A round cover glass was placed on the material and sealed off with chips of paraffin (melting point (600C – 620C). in case of air-bubble formation, the slides are kept in an incubator (temperature more than 600C) for few hours to get rid of the air bubbles.

Slide scanning and Absolute pollen count

The techniques of pollen extraction as described earlier are used for determination of relative frequency of pollen grains and spores only. But the data cannot provide us the density of pollen types with the deposits. The rate of sedimentation of a deposit can be known by doing radiocarbon dating of several sediments. Despite best efforts only a couple of 14C dates could be obtained. Dates on the sub-modern shells turned out to be unacceptable. This is complemented with the introduction of absolute pollen counting method to determine the pollen density of a particular sample. The method used for pollen density count is as follows. (Erdtman 1969; Moore and Webb 1978,Moore et al 1991)

Microscopic observations

Total percentage Pollen count

A known weight of sample was chemically digested in HCl – NaOH – sodium pyrophosphate HF-HCl – glycerin. The processed sub sample in the suspension of glycerin was centrifuged and mounted on slide and pollen grains are counted. Minimum of 200 – 1000 pollen sum was counted and expressed as percentage of the total pollen count. The pollen count was calculated for different Litho unit in the MNS –14 profiles. Total pollen count, percentage frequency, was calculated by standard formula:

(Pollen Count of individual family /Total pollen count in a sample X 100)

Microscopic techniques and photomicrography

Compound Microscope

The C. Z Jenamed binocular research microscope was used for routine investigation and counting. The positions of pollens under observation were noted with the help of platform scale.

Phase Contrast Microscopes

The Leitz DMRB microscope was preferred for critical observations and photo micrographic work. The magnification of the objectives ranged from 40X to 100X. Photomicrographs were taken (Plates 4.3 to 4.25) with Kodak colour film ASA 400 film. Olympus PM –20 was used on selected samples so as to undertake critical photomicrography with Kodak colour film ASA 400 film. Labomed Vision –2000 microscope was used for few samples. The slides were observed at 40X and 100X magnification under oil immersion lense.

Field work studies to explore the modern flora in and around Mansar lake region,

STUDY OF REGIONAL FLORA

The most essential prerequisite to study fossil spores and pollen grains of Quaternary deposits is a adequate knowledge of the regional vegetation and flora and pollen herbarium (palynarium). Therefore, the pollen / spore slides of the extant flora were prepared from a reference collection to facilitate identification of the dispersed fossil grains. A palynarium was a must so as to study the pollen morphology, of plants in the study area. Reconstructing the past environment of Vidarbha- Nagpur region were carried out by referring to both the internal composition of pollen taxa derived from local flora and to numeric relation between particular group and other palynomorphs produced by regional vegetation. The regional vegetation relation do not depend on shape and size of the lake basin, but also on general climatic conditions.

Thus for correct interpretations we tried to establish the general climatic conditions, interpreted from the regional components of vegetation and related pollen spectra. For the same purpose study of surrounding vegetation became mandatory. The total percentage, Dominance of indicator species in the plant assemblage of allochthonous influx of pollen were studied and statistically calculated (Ref. Chapter-II). After this step it was possible to proceed to interpret local factors affecting the deposition of pollen and sediment, which enabled us to separate the regional conditions from the local components. Thus use of regional conditions helped to conclude about the general climatic conditions and applications of local components for interpreting local environment.

Besides, analysis of microfossils from the sediment samples collected from the trench MNS-XIV, at Mansar. Preparation of taxonomical collection of flowering plants with respect to natural flora from reserve forests of Nagpur-Chandrapur-Gadchiroli districts was undertaken for raising palynarium. They are,

i) Pench- Totladoha Tiger reserve – Ramtek (Dist-Nagpur).

ii) Tadoba Andhari Tiger reserve forest (Dist-Chandrapur). (79'o19' N-20o'15'E)

iii) Kolsa – Pipperhetty – Shindevahi (Dist-Chandrapur)

iv) Khadsangi – Chimur (Dist-Chandrapur).

Tadoba represents one of the richest biodiversity in floral and faunal composition in Vidarbha region. The forest type here is southern tropical dry deciduous forest. It is 28 km from Chandrapur. The forest check post is at Agarzari. The center is natural lake covering 300 acres, around which an area of 45 sq. miles has been declared as tiger reserve forest. Now the project is a twin project including area of Andheri and total 116 sq.km area now been called as Tadoba – Andhari tiger project. (79o19'N – 20o15'E)

In order to collect polleniferous material available trees and shrubs species were considered and the systematic plant collection in all seasons including monsoon, late monsoon, winter, early and late summer season was carried out. In early and late monsoon season the monsoon ephemeral flora was collected. The tree species in flowering state were collected as well. Collection of plants its preservation and drying was done as per standard herbarium preparation method. The plants were mounted on standard Herbarium sheets and identified for the botanical name, family, local name etc.(Malhotra and Moorthy,1971,1992,Mahabale ,1966;Naik,1998; Patel,1968; Mirashi, 1954;Almeida et al, 2003,Cook1958, Mathew,1981,Singh and Karthikeyan,2000;Sharma et al,1996.Singh et al 2001

The total number of plant species collected from above mentioned localities comprising 369 genera, 500 species and 97 families. Collection of polleniferous material was taken on clean tissue paper and packets were prepared and labeled properly. Anthers from male and female, spikes, catkin etc. were carefully collected in separate bags without contamination. Cleaned forceps were used to collect the anther specimen. The plant specimens of herbarium were pressed in cartridge drawing absorbent paper in the field to avoid spoilage and fungal attack. Later the plants were dried in press, poisoned and herbarium sheets were prepared. Over 500 plants were collected for enriching herbarium (Table 2.3) and they were identified using standard floras and the confirmation of the plant identification was undertaken at the Botanical Survey of India (BSI)- Western Circle, Pune. The polleniferous material was treated by using standard Acetolysis technique and pollen slides were prepared to raise the palynarium for pollen reference.

Radiocarbon dating

Amongst the physical methods, the 14C dating technique for dating organic remains is still unsurpassed in accuracy. Normally its dating range is 50,000 years for its short half-life years. The technique of 14C have been developed by W.F. Libby (1955).

a. Fossilized shells; bivalves and murex were collected without contamination from different litho units and depth was recorded.
b. The semi carbonized wood pieces, bone pieces charcoal pieces were carefully collected, without contamination; depth was recorded, and kept carefully till further processing.
c. A Minimum sample of 20 g was collected.
d. Box sampling was carried out for AMS dating.
e. Soil samples were also collected for fluorine analysis to predict the approximate age of the soil sample.

Study of magnetic susceptibility and geomagnetism of the soil sample

The soil samples were dried in oven and filled in special vials, labeled to take the readings of frequencies. Magnetic susceptibility was measured with automated Barrington point sensor, at low and high frequency. The frequency readings were taken in the laboratory of Indian Institute of Geomagnetism, (IIGM, Kolaba, Mumbai,). The samples were analyzed for magnetic susceptibility, age of the sediment and co-relation factors in the study area.

Photography of plant –specimens in the field

The area of reserve forests in Chandrapur - Nagpur area was visited to collect herbarium plant specimens and to explore rare plant species. During this exploration it was necessary to document the most unique index taxa. For this very purpose comparable materials and in the process, rare plant species have also been noted, and photo micrography was undertaken with close-up lenses.

In order to include maximum plant species in the virtual Herbarium collection, every flowering season were followed, for three consecutive years. The tree species were in flowering state mostly in March – June and Herbaceous flora, particularly monsoon ephemerals were photographed immediately after first shower in June, as well as in post monsoon period of August - September. Detailed results of Pollen analysis have been illustrated in the subsequent chapter IV , and datasets on analysis of sediments, fossils and meteorological facts have been dealt in chapter V.

4

Analysis and Results of Palynomorphs

Fossil pollen grains, spores and non-polleniferous materials like algae and fungal spores, wood remains, micro charcoal are examined here ,so as to understand the vegetation history of the late Holocene at the Mansar lake. .

Fossil Pollen grains:

Fossil Pollen grains were noted from MNS –XIV. from samples 1 to 25 which comprised of four litho units in total. Pollens were quantified and classified up to family level. The observations were made as per the prescribed description of pollen grains (Nayar,1990,) and taking into due consideration other parameters like shape and sculpturing types (Moore et al .1991, Bhattacharya et al 2006). The fossil pollen grains were compared with the modern pollen grains, which were collected from the natural and protected forest of the study region. A systematic palaynarium was developed as a reference collection of the identification of fossils pollens.

Quantification of fossil pollens from MNS –XIV was classified according to arboreal and nonarboreal plant species along with non-polleniferous palynomorphs.

The following methods have been utilized for appreciating the palaeo-findings.

     a.   Total pollen count
     b.   Total percentage pollen count- litho units wise
     c.   Percentage fossil pollen count of dominant families.

Reference slides: Palynarium

Comparative study of modern and fossil pollen grains.-identification up to Family level. The problem of systematic identification of palynomorphs in minerogenic, oxidizing sediment, even with well-preserved grains has made the pollen spectra, to represent families or at the most generic level. Thus the pollen spectra could not include all pollen taxa though abundantly growing in and around the Mansar lake area.e.g. Families like Rubiaceae, Combretaceae, Verbenaceae, Ebenaceae,Sapotaceae etc. so no specific differentiation could be made The pollen spectrum obtained from Mansar-Nagpur- Chandrapur region is of a much general nature. Thus a refinement in vegetation reconstruction in the way, one may used in peat deposits of temperate region was practically impossible in this study area.

The initial floristic survey of the area under consideration have indicated the likely genera and species of a particular family occurring in the region and there was possibility of their occurrence in the ancient sediments. Neverthless the genera and specific identification were tentatively indicated in the pollen diagram and also in fossil pollen photoplates. Future work is likely to improve upon this aspect.Both herbarium and fresh polliniferous materials were acetoysed. The Acetolysis method as suggested by Erdtman (1956,1969) briefly is as follows.

1) Dry polliniferous material from local herbarium specimen was carefully crushed on a fine brass sieve of 70μ, resting on a funnel set on hard glass centrifuge tube. After each sample the brass sieve was exposed to a flame until it becomes red hot in order to avoid sample contamination.

2) Acetolysis mixture was prepared in a measuring cylinder by slowly   Adding acetic anhydride and Concentrated H_2SO_4 in 9:1 proportion.

3) Then 10 ml of Acetolysis mixture was added drop by drop to test tubes containing crushed material and stirred carefully with a glass rod.

4) After thorough mixing the mixture was heated to boiling point 1000c in water bath for 2-3 minutes, then centrifuged and finally acetolysis mixture was decanted.

5) Little distilled water was added and the sediment was shaken thoroughly, centrifuged and decanted.

6) Process was repeated for 2-3 times.

7) 10ml of glacial acetic acid was added to the tube, content was mixed and centrifuged at 1500 rpm.

8) After decanting Glacial acetic acid (GAA), 10 ml of distilled water was added, and the sediment was washed with distilled water 2 times. The mixture was then sieved through a finely meshed brass net to eliminate foreign particles and again centrifuge and decanted.

9) 50% glycerin was added to the test tube, mixed and centrifuged, and decanted. Then the tubes containing acetolysed pollen/ spore material were kept in inverted condition on filter paper for a few hours in order to dry the material (Erdtman ,1969)

Quantification of fossil pollen grains.

   a) Total pollen count /per sediment sample.
   b) Families representing diagnostic pollens were represented by minimum of 10-15 pollen for poor samples while rich pollen sample count ranged from 200 – 400 –1000 counts.
   c) Total percentage pollen count

Each pollen type is expressed as percentage of the total pollen count in that particular slide. The results are produced in the form of a table as well as in the form of a diagram. These pollen frequency totals from each individual sample are called a " Pollen spectrum" .When a series of these pollen spectra are presented graphically to form a continuous pollen diagram, the percentage of each pollen type within a given level are plotted against the other types.

Distribution of fossil pollen grains

The occurrence, disappearance, and fluctuations in the percentage of fossil pollen types as recorded on the pollen diagram was recorded. . Attempts have been made to reconstruct the palaeovegetational condition that prevailing during the deposition of each layer.Finally conclusion concerning the palaeoenvironment, existed during the estimated period is drawn by inference. This has been utilized for subsequent interpretations of palaeoenvironmental conditions in conjunction with other aspects such as pollen-spore productivity, floristic composition, occurrence of microcharcoals, various microfossils, and radiocarbon dating etc.

Construction of Composite pollen diagram

It was Lennart Von Post (1916,1935.) who first published his result in the form of a "Composite diagram" which has been universally accepted and subsequently modified by scholars.

The vertical axis of the diagram represents depth and the horizontal axis depicts the proportional abundance of the pollen types in which each sample is represented by a horizontal line at the corresponding level. Each horizontal sample line is pollen spectrum for species; hence the diagram consists of a number of spectra from different levels. To demonstrate the change of vegetation, the species are connected from one spectrum to another, by pollen lines. The area comprises all the pollen types that form a part of basic sum.To avoid complicacy , to maintain classification and comparability with other diagrams, the entire diagram is divided into two aspects namely, AP (Arboreal pollen) diagram, including forest trees only, and NAP (Non – Arboreal pollen) diagram depicting non forested species. Both AP and NAP diagrams are constructed in the form of histograms.

The extreme left column of the composite pollen diagrams represents the lithostratigraphic units in sequential order. On its right occurs the column giving the dates of radiocarbon dating. On its further right vegetation / Climatic zones are indicated.

Summary of dominant fossil pollen and spore types

Sr. No.	Family Name	Percentages(%)
1.	Poaceae	83.33
2.	Cyperaceae	58.33
3.	Fabaceae	50
4.	Nymphaeaceae	45.83
5.	Verbenaceae	45.83
6.	Euphorbiaceae	41.66
7.	Acanthaceae	41.66
8.	Sapotaceae	37.5
9.	Myrtaceae	37.5
10.	Convolvulaceae	37.5
11.	Asteraceae	37.5
12.	Amaranthaceae	29.16
13.	Mimosae	29.16
14.	Combretaceae	29.16
15.	Liliaceae	29.16
16.	Nyctaginaceae	20.83
17.	Anacardiaceae	20.83
18.	Chara	20.83
19.	Caesalpiniaceae	16.66
20.	Rutaceae	16.66
21.	Rhamnaceae	16.66
22.	Apocynaceae	16.66
23.	Scrophuliaraceae	16.66
24.	Araceae	16.66

25.	Menispermaceae	8.33
26.	Cucurbitaceae	8.33
27.		
28.	Lamiaceae	8.33
29.	Annonaceae	4.16
30.	Meliaceae	4.16
31.	Bignoniaceae	4.16
32.	Hypoxidaceae	4.16
33.	Orchidaceae	4.16
34.	Fungi (spores)	45.83

Total percentage of fossil pollen count and total fossil pollen count in (MNS –XIV) (Lithounit I-IV)

	Family	Total percentage of fossil Pollen	Total No. of Fossil Pollen count
From Top to Bottom	Litho Unit I (0-40cm)		
1	Amaranthaceae	26.19	71
2	Capparaceae	37.05	21
3	Fabaceae	11.72	258
4	Meliaceae	11.76	4
5	Convolvulaceae	36.49	127
6	Acanthaceae	22.43	59
7	Asteraceae	23.01	58
8	Cyperaceae	12.48	180
9	Poaceae	20.24	282
10	Araceae	37.67	55
11	Nymphaeaceae	34.76	162

	Family	Total percentage of fossil Pollen Count	Total No. of Fossil Pollen count
	Litho Unit II(40-70 cm)		
1	Menispermaceae	66.66	14
2	Amaranthaceae	12.55	34
3	Sapotaceae	47.62	20
4	Malvaceae	15.96	15
5	Euphorbiaceae	35.37	81
6	Fabaceae	6.09	134
7	Caesalpiniaceae	24.39	30
8	Myrtaceae	21.05	4
9	Combretaceae	80	16
10	Rhamnaceae	29.41	5
11	Convolvulaceae	11.49	40
12	Verbenaceae	11.17	20
13	Bombacaceae	100	3
14	Scrophuliaraceae	12.5	8
15	Bignoniaceae	100	6
16	Acanthaceae	28.14	74
17	Asteraceae	9.52	24
18	Liliaceae	16.23	43
19	Cyperaceae	10.61	153
20	Poaceae	1.01	14
21	Araceae	14.38	21
22	Nymphaeaceae	10.94	51
23	Characeae	62.96	17

	Litho Unit III (70-140cm)	% Pollen Count	Total No. of Fossil Pollen
	Family		
1	Annonaceae	83.33	20
2	Menispermaceae	33.33	7
3	Nyctaginaceae	100	2
4	Amaranthaceae	56.8	152
5	Cucurbitaceae	100	2
6	Capparaceae	33.93	19
7	Sapotaceae	55.38	22
8	Tiliaceae	100	141
9	Malvaceae	84.04	79
10	Euphorbiaceae	64.63	148
11	Fabaceae	74.1	1631
12	Mimosae	100	82
13	Caesalpiniaceae	67.48	83
14	Myrtaceae	78.95	15
15	Combretaceae	20	4
16	Rutaceae	100	26
17	Meliaceae	88.24	30
18	Anacardiaceae	100	18
19	Rhamnaceae	70.58	12
20	Apocynaceae	100	3
21	Convolvulaceae	52.01	181
22	Verbenaceae	88.83	159
23	Lamiaceae	100	69
24	Alagnaceae	100	1

| 25 | Simarubaceae | 100 | 2 |

	Litho Unit IV (140-190cm)	% Pollen Count	Total No. of Fossil Pollen
	Family		
1	Annonaceae	16.66	4
2	Amaranthaceae	42.06	14
3	Capparaceae	28.57	16
4	Fabaceae	8.08	178
5	Cyperaceae	5.96	76
6	Poaceae	14.07	196
7	Fungi	63.64	42

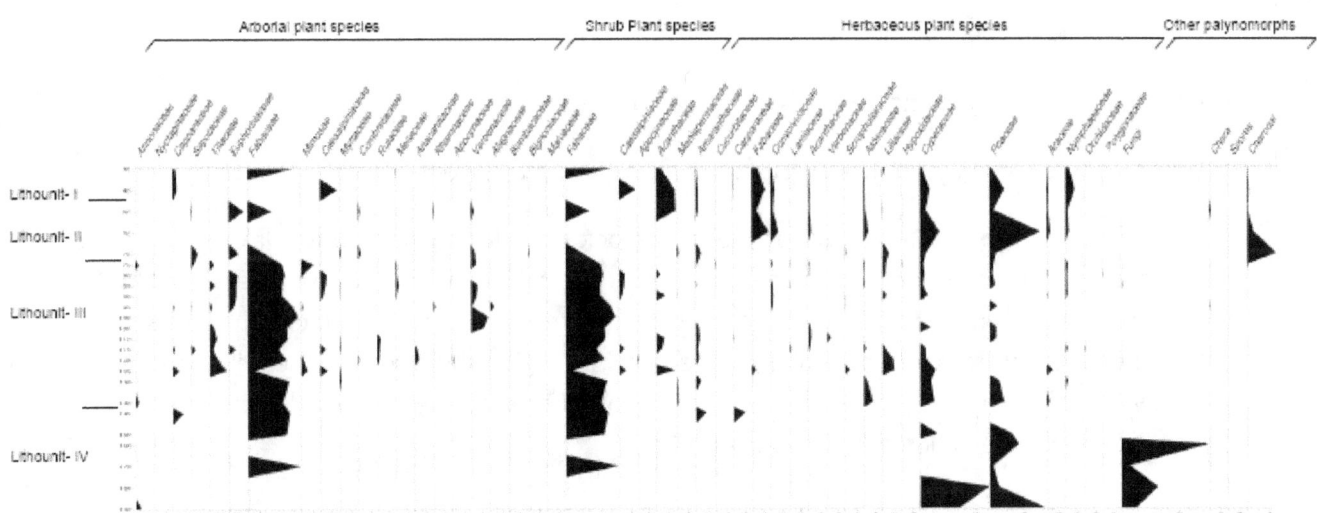

Fig: Pollen Diagram of MNS XIV - Mansar (Nagpur; Central India)

Statistical analysis of percentage pollen count values. MNS-XIV- showing Stability.

Statistical Values	Litho Unit I	Litho Unit II	Litho Unit III	Litho Unit IV
Mean	24.89	31.65	78.07	25.58
S.D.	10.37	29.87	24.52	20.95
% C.V.	41.67	94.37	61.41	81.89

(Less C.V. means more stability and more C.V. means more unstable.)

Conclusion:

1. Average percentage pollen count is highest (78.07) in Litho Unit III proper lacustral phase whereas it is lowest (24.89) in Litho Unit I. Upper Lake drying process.

2. Average percentage pollen count is nearly lowest (25.58) in Litho Unit IV (stream deposits).

3. Percentage Coefficient of variation is minimum in Litho Unit III and therefore Litho Unit III is stable as compared to other Litho Units.

4. Percentage Coefficient of variation in Litho Unit II is maximum and is therefore most unstable as compared to other Litho Units.

Percentage Coefficient of variation = S.D. / Mean *100.

Results from index taxa and pollen assemblege approach

Observation of pollen count from various trenches at Mansar Lake.

In order to fix a reference trench for the palynological studies at the Mansar lake, it was considered necessary to analysis the adjacent trenches in the dried lake bed. Thus soil samples from the following trenches were analyzed for the presence of palynomorphs and other parameters: These samples have been analyzed by standard pollen analysis method with slight modifications. The following trenches give an 'overview' of the sample behavior as well as to understand the potential of the sediments for the presence and preservation of the palynomorphos.

MNS-I (14 samples),

MNS-II (19 samples),

MNS-III (10 samples),

MNS-IV (4 samples),

MNS X (6 samples),

MNS-XIV (24 samples)

MNS-I

Maximum pollen count was observed in sample no 7-14 at the depth of 125 cm. Additional treatment of sodium pyrophosphate after 10 % NaOH was given to the sediments to remove the tenacious clay from the sediment. In sample 13 at the depth of 15-35 cm from the top, presence of macroshells gastropods was noted, so also at the depth of 35 cm. Maximum number of pollen grains were observed in sample number 7 ,at the depth of 110-114 cm., representing maximum biodiversity. And preservation was also good.Though the relative position of these samples is terminal or upper in the profile, they may represent the bottom of ancient lake on which further deposition of sediment did not occur. Sample 1 at the depth of 0-15 cm represents the deepest phase of lake bottom. Presence of macroshells at this depth is also significant and may be contemporary of each other.

MNS-II and MNS-III

These trenches are located to the north of the lake. Trench II was comparatively dry as compared to trench III that was located at the periphery of the present water body. Trench II showed evidences like formation of calcium carbonate nodules Mn precipitation in the lower litho units and formation of rhizoconcretion and iron precipitation in the upper litho units, indicating drying of the lake during late Holocene. The sediments from Trench III were not that productive for palynomorphs count except few Autochthonous palynomorphs and new pedogenisis. Only samples from the uppermost layers show weathered pollen in very few number and diversity.

MNS-IV

This trench is located almost at the center of the lake near to the present water body. This trench is located near an archaeological mound. This trench was dug in as and when the lake was drying in the summer season. Overall the pollen count was fairly notable. At the depth of 45 cm Chara globules were observed for the first time as compared to other trenches.

MNS-X

This trench indicates the deepest phase of the lake (130 cm) as far as the sedimentation indicating deposition of dark brown organic rich sediment. Located in the Southeast region near to the archaeological mound.

It showed a major bulk of brown –black sediment as it was similarly observed in MNS-I, MNS-V, and MNS-VI indicating a similar stratigraphy. All these trenches show palynomorphs in sufficient number.

The sediment was organic, sticky clay, in which percentage of CaCO3 was less, except sample 5 at the depth of 98-100 cm. of MNS-X. To remove the tenacious clay all the samples were treated with 5% sodium hexametaphosphate.

MNS-XIV

This dry trench represents the composite stratigraphical profile of the Mansar lake representing the deepest fluviolacustral phase having perennial water body in the late Holocene. Thus, this trench was studied in detail for pollen analysis so as to understand the holistic view of the lake history as compared to other trenches in detail. This trench was considered very important as it represented datable material like semi-carbonized wood pieces and molluscan shells for 14C dating. The other important finds that make this trench noteworthy for research are the megafossils of carapaces of turtle indicating the ecology of late Holocene indicating semi humid climatic conditions. This trench also represents a general stratigraphic sequence in central part the lake. In all, twenty-four samples were treated by using 60 % HF and sodium hexametaphosphate. The upper level show more carbonate content while lower level contain less carbonate content. The total pollen count of all these samples was minimum 200 to more than 1000 in uppermost samples.

Records of non-pollen palynomorphs (NPP)

The use of non pollen palynomorphs for palaeoenvironmental change is rarely used in palaeoclimate study in India, despite the fact that they occur in palynological preparations of most sediment. Considering their value as palaeoenvironmental indicators, these microscopic objects offer important proxy data for palaeoecological and environmental changes and equally complement palynological data for ecological changes and climate of the past. It has been observed that their implications are significant in pollen poor sediments deposited in semi-arid, Semi-humid, and low-rainfall periods of the Holocene. Further, their occurrence along with palynomorphs of aquatic and terrestrial vascular plants is significant in the reconstruction of lacustral history. Accordingly, an attempt was made to identify the various kinds of NPP recorded from the Late Holocene sediments of the Mansar Lake.

In Mansar, rainfall is medium, approximately 1101 mm and the rate of sedimentation is relatively low. Here preservation of spores and pollen is poor and being intermittently poor pollen sediments, NPP form a significant tool for palaeoenvironmental reconstruction.

Fungal Remains and Spores

Studies on fossil and sub-fossil fungi in India are few and , as their utility in geological aspects has been rarely addressed despite their occurrence in minerogenic sediments, like Mansar lake . Their presence along with spores and pollen of terrestrial vegetation in sediments has gained much attention in view of their utility in palaeofacies de¬termination, interpreting palaeoenvironmental conditions and stratigraphic relationships of sediments. They have been found to be useful and complement palynological data of terrestrial plants. (Limaye et al, 2007)

The relative abun¬dance, host specificity of fungi have significant implications in palaeoenvironmental study. A variety of fungal materials representing spores, and fungal hyphae are present in the palynological preparations in most of the lower and upper samples in the profile MNS-XIV trench. Spores vary from unicellular to multicellular The reduced abundance in Litho unit III of MNS –14 trench sediments, was attributed to a decrease in the rate of soil erosion and related sedimentation in the lake after the establishment of forest.

Vegetative Remains

Organic materials, mainly of woody plant remains, are found in abundance in palynological preparations. Their recovery is better in Litho unit I,II,III,of Mansar-XIV profile and poor in Litho unit IV and V.Fossil pollen grains along with, microcharcoal, microscopic Wood pieces, Trachieds, Vessel elements, Vessel walls with pits are some of the few forms recorded.

Charcoal and Microcharcoal

The jet-black remains in palynological preparations are referred to as microscopic charcoal. Charcoal analysis of sediments along with pollen data from the same cores is used to examine the linkages among climate. Vegetation, fire and sometimes anthropogenic activities in the past. Their occurrence in the sediments may be as a result of natural fires or man-made. Sedimentary layers at the depth of 55cm

From top, of litho unit II (Sample 21,MNS-14) with microcharcoal abundance, suggest evidence of a fire event in the past. Further, microscopic charcoal particles (<100 μm) are carried high up during a fire event and can travel long distances before settling. A record of such particles has provided evidence of regional fires around the Lake region. In sediment sample number 21,(Depth ,55 cm from top of the profile) terrestrial vegetation (pollen, spores, cuticles) is much less and this may be due to paucity of freshwater discharge/weaker monsoon. The prevalence of dry period/poor precipitation and lower humidity can also be attributed due to negli¬gible representation of fungal remains. Nevertheless the higher frequency of pollen, spores, Higher frequency of microscopic charcoal in the prepara¬tion (MNS-XIV, Sample 21,55 cm) indicates forest fire-related events as a result of pre¬vailing dry periods. Further, it may also revealed a period of human-induced forest clearance and burning to obtain openings for cultivation that might have led to significant reduction in forest vegetation around the Mansar lake.

Chara (Algae)

The species of Chara are seasonal and their occurrence depend upon the source of fresh water ,mainly meteoric source .The oogonia of Chara preserved as fossil are characterized by coronular cells. The presence of remains of Chara, a green alga in the deposits at certain levels in the stratigraphic column may be associated with seasonal precipitation, and fresh water conditions. Chara globules were observed in MNS-IV(At 15cm,20cm, 30cm, and 35cm) and MNS-XIV (45 cm),and the relative abundance at these stratigraphic levels ,suggests the palaeoclimate with semi-humid condition and more rainfall.

The overall observation of Non polliniferous palynomorphs in MNS-XIV.

NPP	Characters	Distribution	Palaeoclimatic significance
Chara-Oogonia	Oogonia with spiral bands and coronolar cells.	MNS-IV(15-35 cm),MNS-XIV(45 cm)	Proxy for seasonal water body.
Fungal spores	Chlamydospores, single or Diads.	Litho unit I (0-45 ,cm) and Litho unit IV (130-190 cm)of MNS-XIV.	Human habitation,and Erosion around Mansar lake.
Vegetative remains	Vessel walls ,wood pieces,trachieds,vessels elements.	Litho unit III (70-140 cm) of MNS –XIV.	Allochthonous terrestrial plant species abundance. Suggest semi-humid forest conditions.
Microscopic Charcoal	Jet-black colored particles.	Litho unit-II (55 cm) of MNS-XIV.,sample number 21	Suggest evidence of fire in the past. or local fire,

5

Analysis of Sediments, Megafossils and Metrological Data

Along with other mega fossils like vertebrate and invertebrate fossil remains and shells are also noted. Analysis was also conducted on sediments to understand its chemistry, Magnetic susceptibility and biogeochemical formations, Absolute dates were obtained by 14C dating of semi fossilized wood remains and related archaeological evidences are also noted.

Molluscs analysis

Molluscs are small invertebrate animals with an external shell made of calcium carbonate. Mollusc shells are well preserved in alkaline soils and sediments, from which they can be extracted without chemical pre-treatment. Identification is generally to species level. The species composition of land snail assemblages is largely dependent on climate and on local habitat, especially vegetation cover. During the terminal Pleistocene and early Holocene land snails found in colluvial and similar sequences closely mirror vegetation changes over the same time period (Kerney, 1977). Later in the Holocene land snails have proved especially valuable in archaeological contexts, such as soils buried beneath burial mounds (Evans, 1972). Species which are shade tolerant or intolerant provide good indicators of whether the vegetation was formerly wooded or open, and hence of forest clearance and regeneration.

Molluscs are also found in aquatic and marine environments, as bivalves like mussels as well as gastropods (snails) Most freshwater molluscs, having wide climatic tolerances, instead provide an indication of local aquatic conditions; for example, whether the water was moving or stagnant (Lozek, 1986). Preliminary Report on the study of Freshwater Molluscan Shells from Mansar Lake Dist. Nagpur, Maharashtra) (Courtesy- Dr.Arati Deshpande-Mukharjee Deccan college Pune)

Freshwater shells from the following trenches of Mansar lake samples were collected by dry sieving method for detailed studies.

The following samples were analyzed:

No:16-MNSII-Depth30cm

No:3-MNSIII-Depth50-60cm.

No:4-MNSIII-Depth60-70cm

No:5- MNS III- Depth 72-80cm

Observations:

1) All the samples contained only gastropod shells. These show good preservation and are complete.

2) The shells have lost their original colour and have a chalky appearance.

3) Absence of bivalve shells is evident. A majority of the shells are very small in size ranging from 2 mm to 10 mm. These represent juvenile individual.

4) A total of five species arc identified in the overall sample. These have bee identified only to the generic level.

1.   Lymnaca spp.

2.   Gyraulus spp.

3.   Melania striatella spp.

4.   Bellamya spp.

5.   Thiara spp.

Some basic ecological information from the shells is possible.

All the species represented are typical freshwater molluscs inhabiting ponds and lakes. These species occur as large assemblages within water bodies. They either lie buried within soft muddy bottoms or can be found attached to vegetation. Lymnaca sp. indicates presence of vegetation in the lake as these are often associated with them. Most of these species have a tendency to burrow into the soft mud in times of desiccation of lake or ponds during summer season. At the onset of favorable wet conditions like the rainy season, they get revived.

Hence presence of juvenile shells speaks for this sort of phenomenon in sub- modern time. Probably these shells did not get a chance to grow into adult individuals because of severe desiccation. In such cases if deposition is quick an entire assemblage gets deposited. Here the shells show that after death they were deposited under favorable conditions such as a stable calm aquatic environment.

It also reveals that annual shrinking and filling up of the lake caused shells to accumulate and perish in large numbers. However, a further detailed study is essential for inferring the depositional history of the lake using these molluscan shells.

Carapaces: The megafossil remains of fresh water turtle has been observed and collected at the depth of 48-90 cm in MNS-XIV indicating deep water phase.

Wild bore bones: Semifossilized bones of wild bore (Sus scrofa) has been recovered at the depth of 125 cm in MNS – I, indicating thick forest cover around Mansar lake.

Root nodules: Fossilized root nodules were found at thedepth of 163 cm, in lithounit IV of MNS-XIV, indicating dry climatic conditions. Because roots become nodular to store water, a xerophytic character.

PROFILE - MNS - XIV - STATIGRAPY

Litho unit	Depth in cm	Sediment	Sample no.	Position of sample	Pollen status	Charcoal	Shell	Description and other objects.
LU-I	0							
	10		26	———	✓	✗	✓	
0-40	20		25	———	✓	✗	✓	New Soil
	30		24	———	✓	✗	✓	
	40		23	———	✓	✗	✓	
	50		22	———	✓	✗	✓	Black Soil with cracks
LU-II	60		21	———	✗	✗	✗	
40-70	70		20	———	✓	✗	✗	
LU-III	80		19 18	——— ———	✓ ✓	✗ ✗	✗ ✗	
40-140	90		17 16	——— ———	✓ ✓	✗ ✗	✗ ✗	
	100		15 14	——— ———	✓ ✓	✗ ✗	✗ ✗	Compact Black Clay
	110		13 12	——— ———	✓ ✓	✗ ✗	✗ ✗	
	120		11 10	——— ———	✓ ✓	✗ ✗	✗ ✗	
	130		9 8	——— ———	✓ ✓	✗ ✗	✗ ✗	
	140		7 6	——— ———	✓ ✓	✓ 130-140cm ✗	✗ ✗	Charcoal
LU-IV	150		5	———	✓	✗	✗	
140-190	160		4	———	✓	✗	✗	Limonotized sand
	170	14 C -164 cm	3	———	✓	✗	✗	14 C dating sample-164 cm 3320-3000 yrs BP
	180		2	———	✓	✗	✗	
	190	14 C -190 cm	1	———	✓	✗	✗	14 C dating sample-190 cm 1870-1630 yrs BP
	200							
	210	WATER LEVEL						

Semi corbonised wood pieces

▨	BLAACK SOIL	✓ PRESENT
▨	CLAY	✗ ABSENT
▨	SAND	

POLLEN RECORD OF VEGETATION CHANGE
IN FOREST ZONE AROUND MANSAK LAKE

Litho unit	Depth in cm	Composite Statigrapy - MNS	Yr. B. P.	Dominant Flora	Subdominant Flora	Reconst-ruted Flora
LU-I 0-40	0 10 20 30 40		342.8	Amaranthaceae Fabaceae Meliaceae Convolvulaceae Acanthaceae Asteraceae Cyperaceae Poaceae Araceae Nymphaeaceae	Capparaceae Verbenaceae Euphorbiaceae	Grasses Herbs Sedges Thining of Forest
LU-II 40-60	50 60			20, 5, 8, 22, 16, 9, 12, + Characeae (Algae)	3, 7, 9, 19, 18,+ Acanthaceae, Asteraceae Cyperaceae, Poaceae Araceae, Nymphaeaceae Bombacaceae, Bignoniaceae	Semi-arid Forest
			514.2	Minimum % Pollen Count		
LU-III 60-130	70 80 90 100 110 120 130		685.6 1114	1) Annonaceae 2) Nyctaginaceae 3) Amaranthaceae 4) Cucurbitaceae 5) Sapotaceae 6) Tiliaceae 7) Malvaceae 8) Euphorbiaceae 9) Fabaceae 10) Mimosae 11) Caesalpiniaceae 12) Myrtaceae 13) Rutaceae 14) Meliaceae 15) Anacardiaceae 16) Rhamnaceae 17) Apocynaceae 18) Verbenaceae 19) Lamiaceae	20) Menispermaceae 21) Capparaceae 22) Combretaceae 23) Rutaceae 24) Convolvulaceae 25) Alagnaceae 26) Simarubaceae	Woodland ↑ Stable Tropical Semi - humid Forest ↓
LU-IV 130-180	140 150 160 170 180		14C Date	Annonaceae Amaranthaceae Capparaceae Fungi spores Fern spores	Fabaceae Cyperaceae Poaceae	Few Tress Spcies + Herbaceous Flora ↑ Unstable transitional vegetation ↓
LU-V 180-200	190 200 210	WATER LEVEL	1630 1714			Collurial Gravel

☐ BLAACK SOIL   ✓ PRESENT

☐ CLAY

☐ SAND   ✗ ABSENT

Dating of sediments

One of the most frequent questions a palaeobotanist has to concern is the method for dating sediments containing fossil plants and animals. Present knowledge is based on a long series of efforts to date the ages of various rocks. At the present time. The best absolute dating involves the use of naturally occurring radioactive isotopes contained in various minerals that make up a rock. These radioactive isotopes are sometimes referred to as "Geological clocks."

Radiocarbon dating

Amongst the physical methods, the 14C dating technique for dating organic remains is still unsurpassed in accuracy. Normally its dating range is 50,000 years for its short half-life. W.F. Libby in1955 has developed the technique of 14C. (Lee, 1995)

• Fossilized shells, bivalves, murex were collected without contamination from different litho units and depth was recorded.

• The semi carbonized wood pieces, bone pieces charcoal pieces were carefully collected, without contamination; depth was recorded, and kept carefully till further processing.

• For 14C dating result, standard Performa from BSIP – Lucknow was filled and sent with all the necessary details of the sample. Minimum sample required for the 14C dating as per BSIP is 20g.

• Box sampling was done , for AMS dating to be carried out in future

• Soil and sediment samples were collected for Fluorine analysis to appreciate the relative age of the samples. age of the soil sample. This process was carried out in the chemistry laboratory of Dept of Archaeology, Deccan College, Pune.

^{14}C dating:MNS-XIV (Mansar)

Sample No. and Depth in cm	BS No.	Age of the sample based on the value of half life = 5570± 30 yrs.	Calibrated age range (yrs. BP)
MNS-XIV	2088	2970± 80	3320-3000
164 cm			
MNS-XIV 190 cm	2089	1830± 80	1870-1630

Two shell samples for radiocarbon dating were sent to Birbal Sahani Institute of Palynology; Lucknow. The first sample came from trench MNS-I, depth 20-45 cm. The second shell sample was obtained by clubbing together the molluscan species from stratigraphically comparable trenches MNS-IV and MNS-VI to make 20 gm by weight as per the norms of the laboratory. The radiocarbon assay, however, suggested them to be of modern age. Obviously, such type of thing could happen because of after-effect of Second World War bombing phenomenon.

Unfortunately, we did not have access to Lead- Cesium dating of the younger deposits. On stratigraphical consideration and field evidence, we tentatively suppose them to be of sub-modern period.

Study of magnetic susceptibility and geomagnetism of the soil sample:

The sediment particles have inbuilt magnetic properties that often vary with the changes in the lithogenic fractions of them and the changes are controlled by multiple factors. Basically environmental magnetism is a measurement of several such mineral fractions from the sediments/ rocks. Magnetic properties of natural materials depend upon the formation, transport, deposition and transformation of magnetic minerals controlled by environmental condition and geological process (Basavaiah and Khadkikar, 2004; Deotare et al .2004). The mineral magnetic records therefore provide a sensitive indicator of changing sediment sources. This can be related with the sediment characters, sedimentary process, climatic conditions and the biological activity by the microorganisms.

Reconstructing past erosion rates in a lake catchments

Lakes act as receptacles for materials, which are removed from their catchments, the majority of which are deposited in the lakebed. In order to overcome the problem of differences in the rate of sedimentation over the bed it is necessary to take multiple cores, typically one per 0.5-1.0 ha of the lake surface. These cores need to be correlated with one another by methods such as magnetic susceptibility. Using magnetic susceptibility profiles it is possible to establish which cores have fast and which have slow sedimentation rates, and to select for detailed dating those with representative sediment profiles. Once dated and correlated, accumulation rates over the lake can be established for different time periods in the past. The mean rate of sediment accumulation over the whole lakebed (usually recorded as gm/cm2/yr) may be used as a measure of the rate of sediment influx into the lake, which in turn can be converted into mean catchments erosion rate (Dearing, 1986).

The study of magnetic susceptibility –

The analysis of such sediment was of particular value because the exposed profiles at Mansar lake bed were used to reconstruct the past vegetation history, climatic conditions, as well as also could provide the soil erosion rate and sediment influx.

Mansar lake is relatively shallow, situated in an area of predominantly farming. We tried to detect the past erosion rates of soil, by taking 22 trenches, approximately of 2.50 meter deep sediment profile set over the dried lake surface. The details of Mansar lake are as follows,

- Name- Mansar lake

- Geographic Location- 210 20'N-70015'E

- Lake area- 59.69 hectare

- Water depth- 11 feet

- Sediment thickness- 2.50 m

- Maximum sediment date- c.1870-c 1630 yrs. B.P.

In order to conduct magnetic susceptibility at the lake Mansar sample from the following trenches were taken for analysis so as to have a correlation between the results obtained.

TRENCHES,

1.   MNS-I

2.   MNS-II

3.   MNS-III

4.   MNS-IV

5.   MNS-V

6.   MNS-VI

Laboratory Methods

After description and photography of the sampling measurements of magnetic susceptibility of MNS-I to MNS-VI sediment samples were measured. The age model couldn't be established since only one valid 14C date is available.c.1870-c .1630 yrs.B.P. The overall straightygraphy of Mansar lake has been given in the composite profile. The position of trenches in the dried lakebed of Mansar Lake is shown. The soil samples were dried in oven and filled in special vials, labeled to take the readings of frequencies. Magnetic susceptibility was measured with automated Barrington point sensor, at low and high frequency. The frequency readings were taken in the laboratory of IGM, Kolaba, Mumbai. The data have been analysed for magnetic susceptibility, influx of the sediment and co-relation with pollen records, in the study area. Although the data set is preliminary and mainly suffers from lack of high-resolution pollen data and detail geochemical investigations, it was possible to infer few palaeoenvironmental and palaeoclimatic conclusions.The main change recorded was an increase in erosion rate during recent time. Study of historical records has shown that it has happened with an expansion of ploughed land in the study area. The agricultural intensification had increased the soil losses from the catchments.

The conclusions are as follows,(After studying the sediments of MNS-I to MNS-VI w.r.t. frequency amplitude of magnetic susceptibility)

The profile MNS-I, MNS-II, and MNS-III showed a progressive increase in sediment accumulation, while MNS-IV, MNS-V,and MNS-VI, represented the low sedimentation rate, a low energy lake, except after 400 yrs B.P.with increased land use. Further in this catchments soil losses under recent mining activity and agriculture land use represent increased rate as compared with that under early Holocene forest cover.Without doubt, land degradation has occurred in Mansar area in recent times due to population growth and agrasion pressure.

Litho unit I (0-40 cm)-The minerogenic input is increased, characterized by high amplitude of frequencies in magnetic susceptibility, and pollen record is characterized by rise in NAP amounts and drop in semi-humid pollen percentage. Increase of Poaceae ,Cyperaceae, Chenopodiaceae,and Amarantaceae pollen, reflects a climatic condition with high precipitation rate and more sediment influx due to soil erosion. Autochthonous biogenic deposits have increasingly diluted the allochthonous pollen influx during last 50 years. It may be due to Eutrophication.

Litho unit II (40-60 cm)- It represents a short period with high minerogenic input ,indicated by high levels of amplitude in magnetic susceptibility. The pollen record shows a remarkable increase in NAP and decrease in semi-humid plant species . The low resolution of preliminary pollen record did not allow recognition of climatic change, because there is no pollen sample between Litho unit I and Litho unit II(sample 21,MNS-XIV,at 55 cm) .The occurrence of Microscopic charcoal have indicated occurrence of local fire in the study area. This observation point to a major climatic deterioration in last 500 years.

Litho unit III- (60-130 cm)-The amplitude of magnetic susceptibility is very low. It means the minerogenic input was very low and there was increased clay percentage representing semi-humid climate with high fluvial runoff and a dense semi humid forest cover. The lake level should have been higher than in litho units I,II and IV, since minerogenic input was low. It represent deepest part of the lake. Formation of carbonate nodules hints for the precipitation of carbonates in shallow peripheral zone of the lake. It indicates existence of a humid and warm climate. The pollen records shows maximum biodiversity in AP pollen count, indicators of semi- humid, to humid climatic conditions, lasted more or less invariable until the onset of terminal Holocene period.

Litho unit IV and V-130-250 cm)-The sediment of Litho unit IV and V are characterized by high frequency value with high amplitude changes of magnetic susceptibility. The palaeoenvironmental conditions seems to be more variable with maximum Holocene summer monsoon ,maximum fluvial runoff from the tributary coming in the Mansar lake.(Pench river valley-Nagpur). The pollen record with more

Poaceae and Cyperaceae with few arboreal pollen and fungal spores, which are indicator of primary forest as well as humid climatic conditions, indicate gradual spread of grassland with influx of plant remains, and scattered minerogenic particles mainly MnO2 concretions, from the surrounding area after damming of the Mansar lake.

Magnetic susceptibility frequency records

MNS-I	DEPTH(CM)	LF	DEPTH(CM)	HF
1	180-195	11.8	180-195	10.2
2	135-145	13.2	135-145	12.1
3	95-105	11.5	95-105	10.7
4	60-65	11.5	60-65	10.7

MNS-II	DEPTH(CM)	LF	DEPTH(CM)	HF
1	210-220	9.63	210-220	9.1
2	200-205	15.8	200-205	15
3	190-195	13.5	190-195	13
4	180-175	10.2	180-175	9.9
5	155-160	11.2	155-160	10.7
6	145-150	10.4	145-150	10.2
7	135-140	10.7	135-140	10.3
8	125-130	10.7	125-130	10.1
9	115-120	11.3	115-120	1.2
10	105-110	9.63	105-110	9.4
11	95-100	12.2	95-100	11.9
12	85-90	10.6	85-90	10.2
13	75-80	10.6	75-80	10.3
14	65-70	10.1	65-70	9.8

15	55-60	10.3	55-60	10.1
16	45-50	9.58	45-50	9.4
17	35-40	8.38	35-40	7
18	15-20	10.9	15-20	10.1
19	0-10	11.3	0-10	11.2

MNS-III	DEPTH(CM)	LF	DEPTH(CM)	HF
1	95-100	11.7	95-100	9.7
2	85-90	14.6	85-90	11.7
3	75-80	12	75-80	11.4
4	65-70	11.8	65-70	10.5
5	55-60	10.2	55-60	8.6
6	45-50	9.4	45-50	7
7	35-40	8.1	35-40	6.6
8	25-30	8.3	25-30	7.1
9	15-20	8.7	15-20	7.7
10	0-10	7.9	0-10	6.9

MNS-IV	DEPTH(CM)	LF	DEPTH(CM)	HF
	6	68.6	6	67.8

MNS-IV	DEPTH(CM)	LF	DEPTH(CM)	HF
	8	75.1	8	74.8
	10	14.3	10	13.2
	12	17.9	12	16.9
	14	13.2	14	12.2
	16	14	16	13.2
	18	11.9	18	10.3
	20	13.1	20	11.9
	22	12.4	22	11.5
	24	11.8	24	10.7
	26	17.7	26	16.8
	28	10.8	28	9.8
	30	10.7	30	10.1
	32	11	32	10.3
	34	11.5	34	10.8
	36	11.3	36	10.7
	38	11.3	38	10.8
	40	11.1	40	10.5
MNS-IV	DEPTH(CM)	LF	DEPTH(CM)	HF
	42	11.1	42	10.5
	44	11.4	44	10.9
	46	11.2	46	9.8
	48	11.3	48	9.8
	50	11.3	50	9.7
	52	12.8	52	9.7
	56	13.7	56	12.2
	58	12.4	58	11.1

MNS-IV	DEPTH(CM)	LF	DEPTH(CM)	HF
	60	14.4	60	13.1
	62	13.1	62	12.1
	64	12.9	64	11.4
	66	12.1	66	10.8
	68	12.5	68	11.3
	70	12.1	70	11.3
	72	12.5	72	11.8
	74	13	74	12.5
	76	11.3	76	11.2
	78	11.1	78	10.6
	80	12.3	80	12.1
	82	11.4	82	11
	84	11.2	84	10.9
	86	10.7	86	9.5
	88	10.7	88	10.4
	90	10.5	90	10.2
	92	10.6	92	10.3
	94	10.3	94	10
	96	9.08	96	8.9
	98	9.5	98	9.2
	100	11.3	100	10.5
	102	11.5	102	11.1
MNS-IV	DEPTH(CM)	LF	DEPTH(CM)	HF
	104	10.6	104	10.3
	106	10.9	106	10.5
	108	10.5	108	10.1

	110	10.6	110	10.3
	112	10.5	112	10.3
	114	11.5	114	11
	116	41.5	116	40.8
	118	11.1	118	10.8
	120	11.1	120	10.7
	122	11.2	122	11.9
	124	13.5	124	13.1
	126	12.5	126	12.1
	128	11.8	128	11.6
	130	11.9	130	11.7
	132	13.1	132	12.8
	134	13.2	134	12.9
	136	13.3	136	13.1
	138	14.2	138	13.9
	140	14.7	140	14.2
	142	13.8	142	13.5
	144	15.4	144	14.9
	146	14.9	146	14.4
	148	13.3	148	13
	150	13.4	150	13
	152	17.6	152	16.9
	154	18.7	154	18.1
	156	14	156	13.7
	158	19	158	18.2
	160	19.2	160	18.4

	162	15.1	162	14.9

MNS-IV	DEPTH(CM)	LF	DEPTH(CM)	HF
	164	12.6	164	12.2
	166	15.7	166	15
	168	12	168	11.8
	170	14	170	13.6
	172	13	172	12.7
	174	18.2	174	17.9

MNS-V	DEPTH(CM)	LF	DEPTH(CM)	HF
	0	12.3	0	11.6
	2	12.5	2	12.3
	5	12.8	5	12.3
	6	14	6	13.5
	10	13.7	10	13.2
	12	12.8	12	12.6
	15	12.4	15	12
	18	13.8	18	10.8
	20	11.9	20	11.8
	22	12.5	22	12.1
	25	12	25	11.7
	28	11.6	28	11.1
	30	11.5	30	11
	34	12.2	34	9
	37	9.83	37	8.8

	DEPTH(CM)		DEPTH(CM)	
	40	11.7	40	10.3
	44	11.9	44	9.5
	48	11	48	8.4
	50	10.8	50	10
	52	12.3	52	11
	55	12.5	55	11.3
	58	12	58	10.8

MNS-V	DEPTH(CM)	LF	DEPTH(CM)	HF
	60	12.3	60	11.1
	62	12.6	62	10.1
	64	10.3	64	9.4
	66	7.48	66	7
	68	8.38	68	7.8
	70	9.83	70	9
	72	10.1	72	9.9
	74	7.43	74	6.9
	76	9.43	76	7.9
	78	9.63	78	7.5
	80	11.9	80	9.3
	82	9.68	82	7.4
	84	8.88	84	6.2
	86	9.15	86	6.8
	88	9.35	88	6.9
	90	9.88	90	8.2
	92	5.23	92	4

MNS-V	DEPTH(CM)	LF	DEPTH(CM)	HF
	94	6.58	94	5.9
	96	7.33	96	6.2
	98	8	98	6.5
	100	8.33	100	6.9
	102	9.3	102	7.7
	104	6.13	104	5
	106	8.18	106	7
	108	8.45	108	7.4
	110	8.88	110	7
	112	10.6	112	8.7
	114	7.75	114	5.9
	116	7.23	116	5.7
	118	6.43	118	5.4
MNS-V	DEPTH(CM)	LF	DEPTH(CM)	HF
	120	6.53	120	5.5
	122	11.4	122	10.1
	124	7.35	124	6.1
	126	8.85	126	7.6
	128	12.9	128	11.7
	130	12.1	130	11.1
	132	10	132	8.9
	134	10.8	134	9.9
	136	6.28	136	5.4
	138	9.73	138	9
	140	10.7	140	9.7

MNS-VI	DEPTH(CM)	LF	DEPTH(CM)	HF
	3	67.4	3	65.9
	7	74	7	72.1
	10	67.6	10	66.1
	13	68.1	13	66.5
	17	49	17	47.9
	20	10	20	9.9
	23	12.3	23	12.1
	27	23.3	27	22.7
	30	10.1	30	9.9
	33	9.73	33	9.5
	37	11.6	37	11.3
	40	10.4	40	10.3
	43	11.6	43	11.4
	47	12.1	47	12.1
	50	10.4	50	10.32
	53	13.2	53	13
	57	10.3	57	10
MNS-VI	DEPTH(CM)	LF	DEPTH(CM)	HF
	60	8.8	60	8.5
	63	11	63	10.5
	67	10.9	67	10.7
	70	11.9	70	11.7
	73	11.1	73	10.9
	77	11.2	77	11.2
	80	13.1	80	12.9

	83	11.2	83	11
	87	9.5	87	9.3
	90	9.03	90	8.9
	93	10.4	93	10.2
	97	9.03	97	8.9
	100	9.8	100	9.5
	103	9.93	103	9.7
	107	8.2	107	8
	110	9.58	110	9.4
	113	9.3	113	9.1
	117	9.6	117	9.3
	120	10.4	120	10.2
	123	10.4	123	10.1
	127	9.28	127	9
	130	10.6	130	10.4
	137	10.4	137	10.1
	140	9.35	140	9.1
	143	10.7	143	10.2
	147	10.7	147	10.5
	150	10.2	150	9.8
	153	9.1	153	8.9
	157	41.3	157	40
	160	9.9	160	9.6
	163	10.6	163	10.3
	167	10.4	167	10.3
	170	6.4	170	6.2

Magnetic susceptibility curves MNS-I and MNS –II

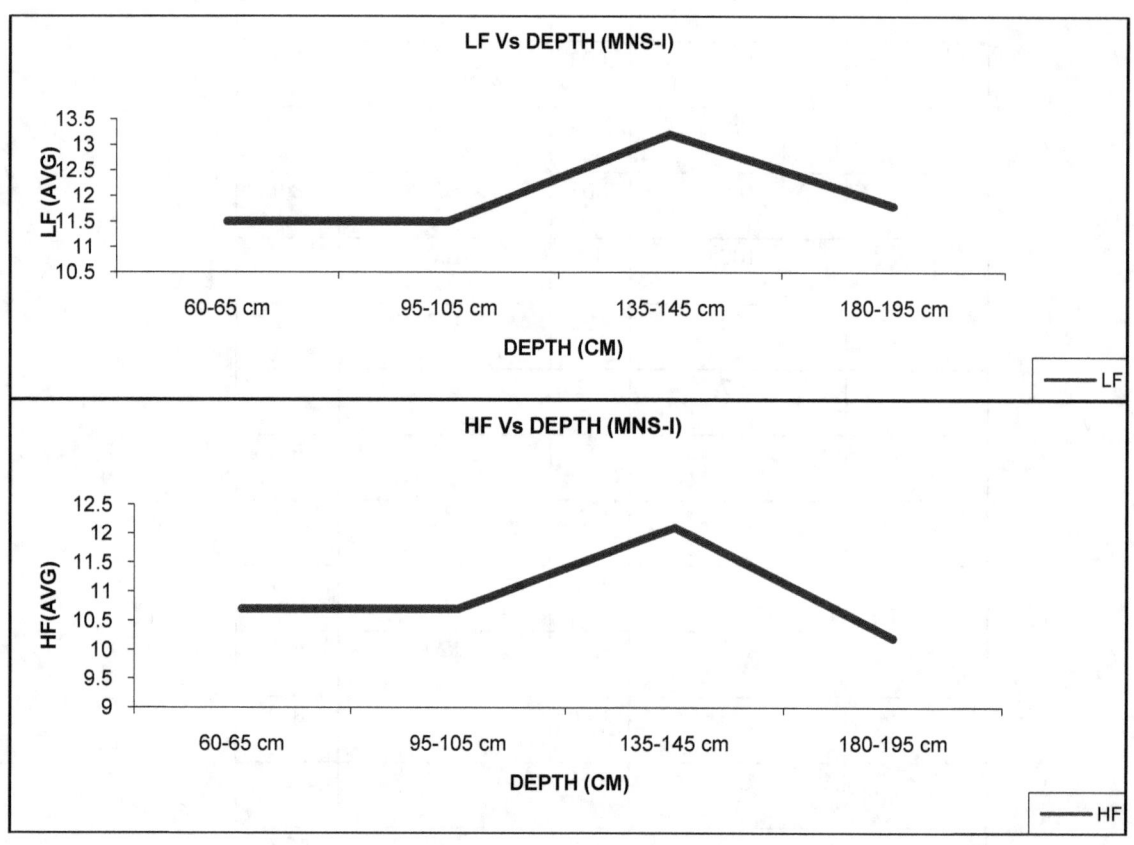

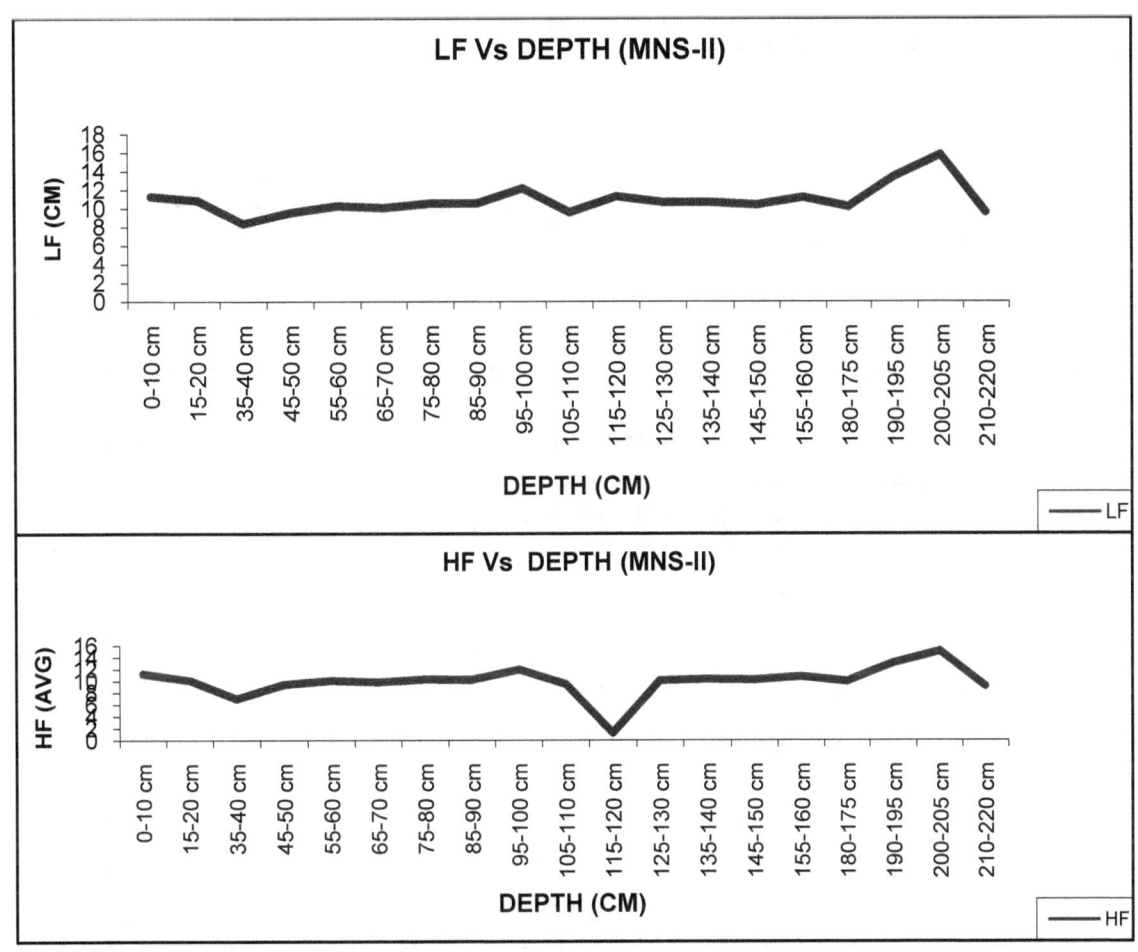

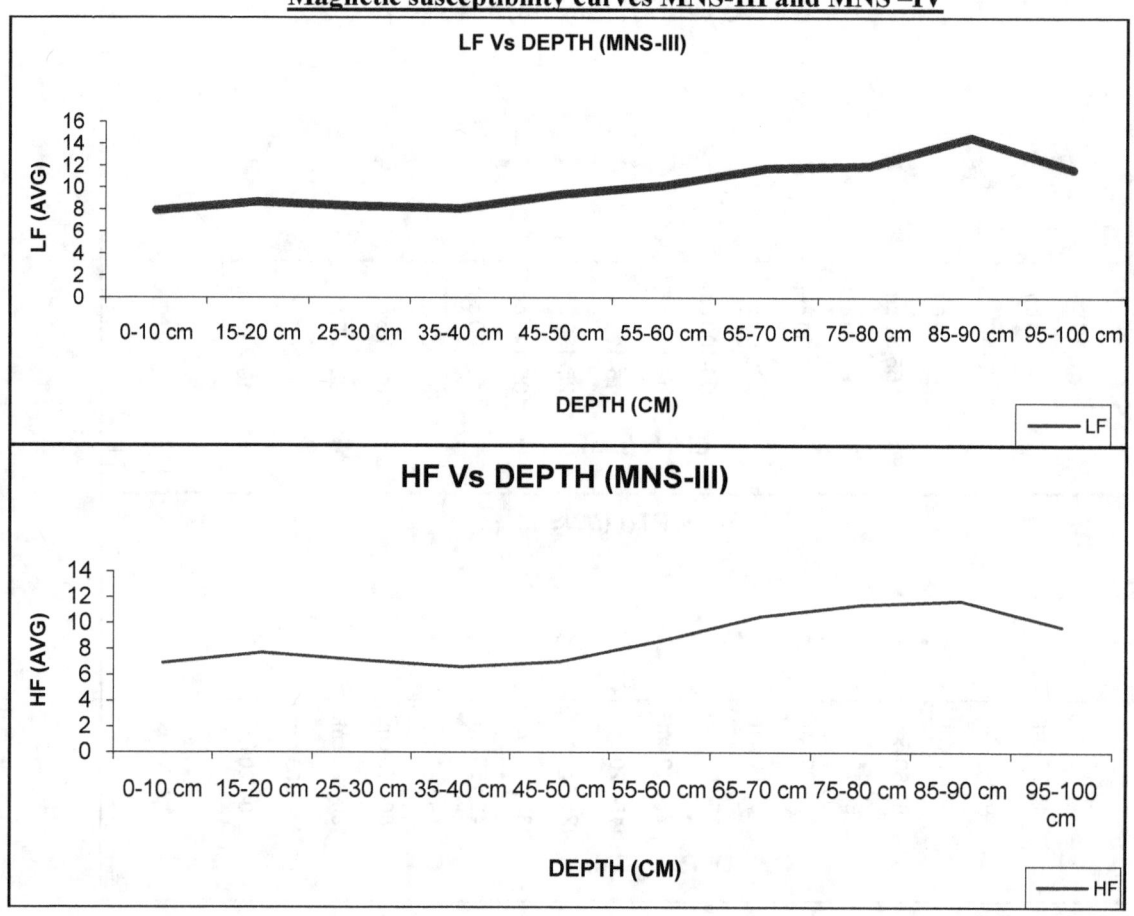

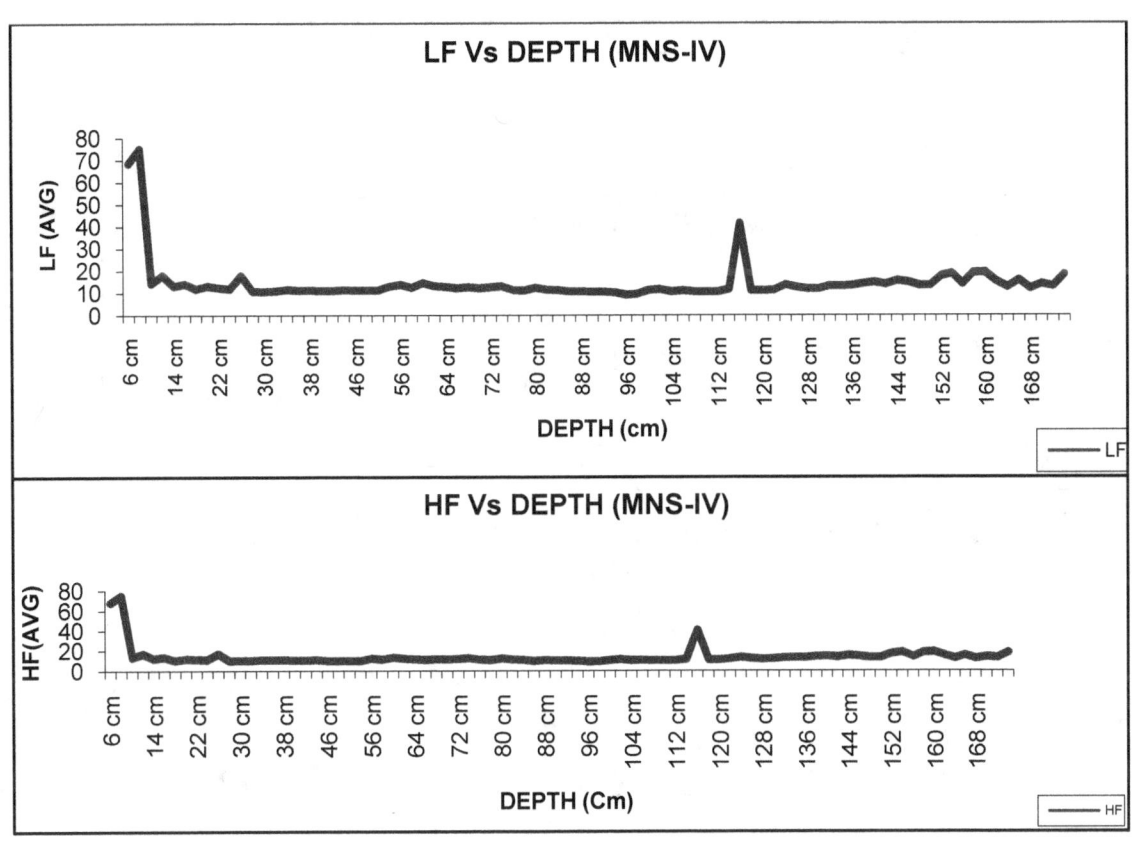

LF Vs DEPTH (MNS-IV)

HF Vs DEPTH (MNS-IV)

Magnetic susceptibility curves MNS-V and MNS –VI

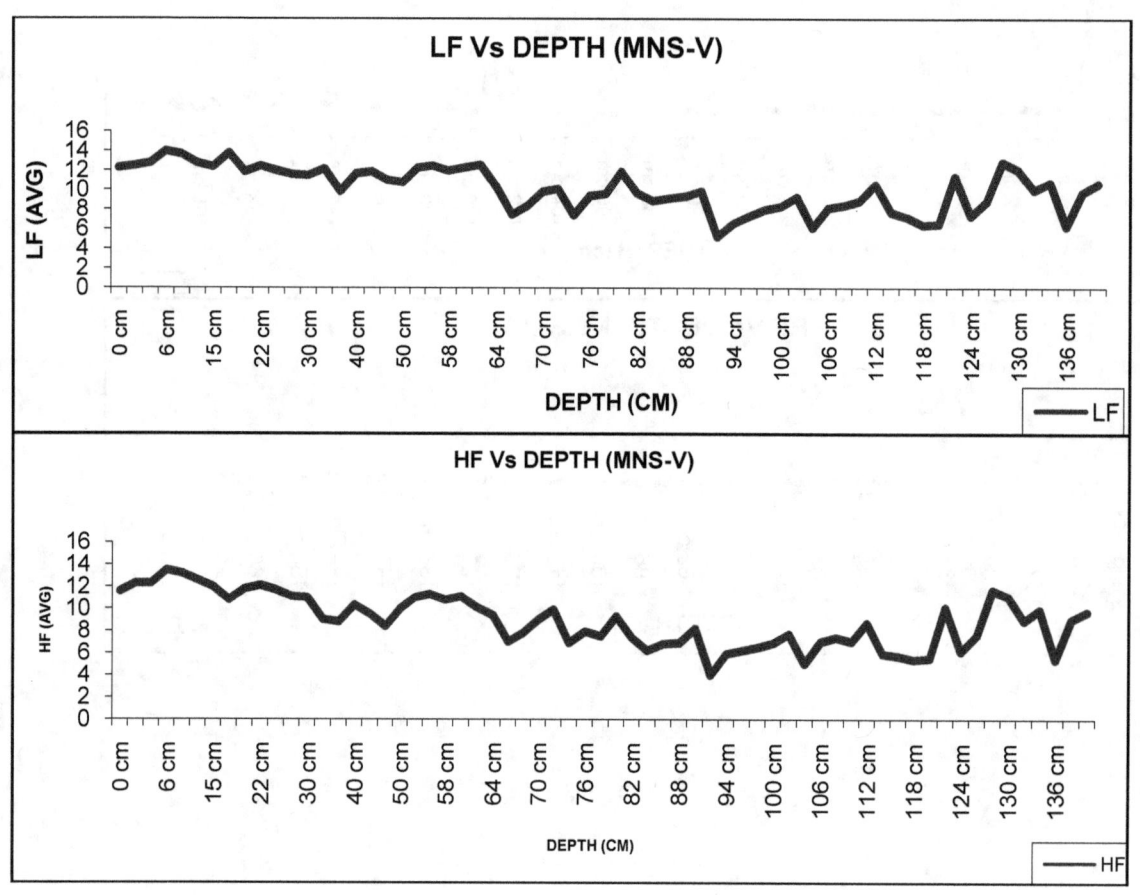

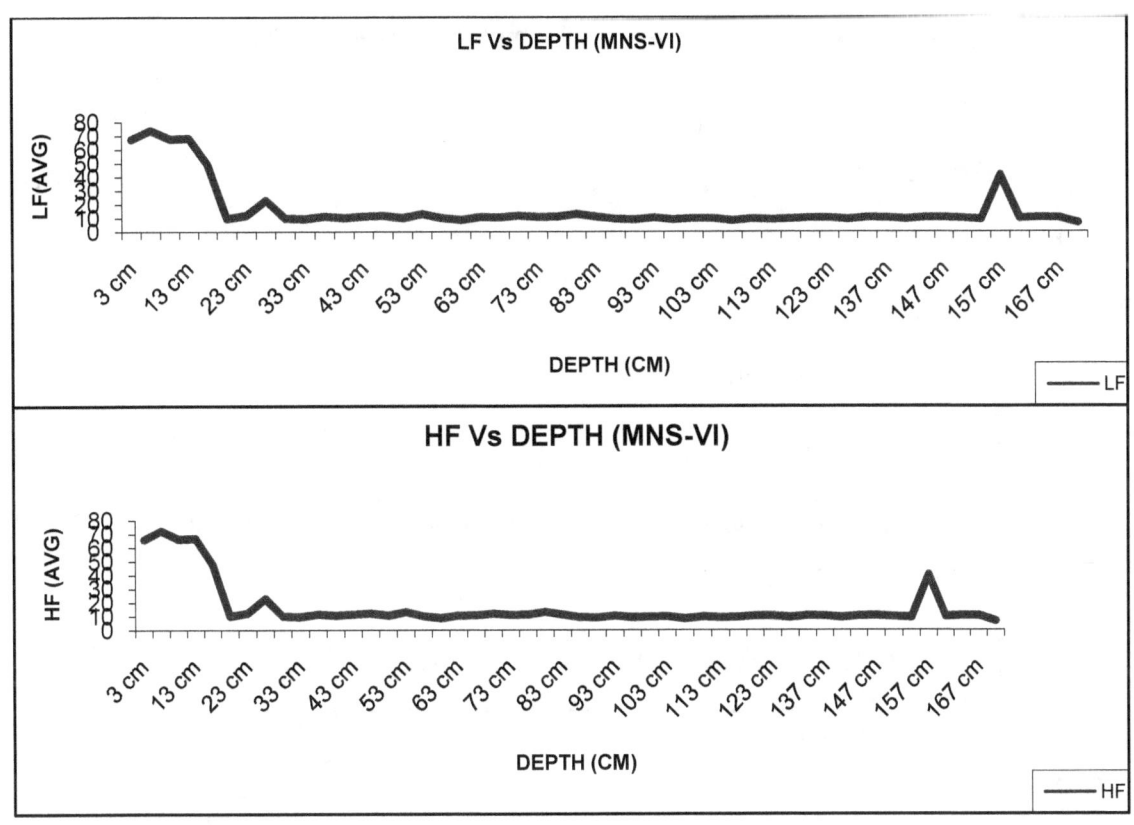

Physico-chemical properties of soil sample from Mansar lake

11P20061050001

Receipt No 8251559

Date   8/5/2007

SOIL REPORT   MNS-14 (MANSAR)

No	Property		
A	Chemical property	Observation	Explanation
1	pH	6.33	Slightly Acidic
2	EC(Electrical conductivity)	0.49	Normal
3	O.C (%)	0.61	
4	N (Kg)		
5	P_2O_5 (Kg)	32.28	Medium
6	K_2O(Kg)	1288.1	Excess
7	Ca (%)	70.35	
8	Mg (%)	24.45	
9	Na (%)	3.26	
10	$CaCO_3$ (%)	4.13	Normal
B	Physical property		
		Observation	Explanation
1	a) Sand (%)	43.27	
	b)Clay Loam	23.65	Clay Loam
	c)Clay (%)	32.81	
2	Moisture (%)	13.98	

3	MWHC (%)	52.69	
4	Particle density (Gm/CC)	1.91	
5	Density	1.16	
6	Porosity (%)	59.1	
7	Size (%)	26.15	

Govt. of India

Agriculture Division (MAHARASHTRA)

Soil sample Analysis Laboratory PUNE

www.maharashtra.gov.in

MSSTL

Biogeo chemical formations in Mansar lake sediments.

At the Mansar lake 22 trenches were dug from various location of the lake. Taking into consideration the geological and lake hydrological aspects, the entire lake sedimentation was divided into five litho units.In general the trenches show following sediment deposition.

LITHOUNIT I - Uppermost layer - 0-40 cm- upper most Black soil (20 cm) with grass cover, vertical cracks observed, Full of modern gastropod shells rootlets, brick bats, pot shreds (often non-diagnostic pieces), Terracotta beads, etc were observed.

LITHOUNIT II - 40-60 cm- grayish brown clayey silt, well developed block; peds, iron rhizoconcretions at 45cm in MNS -14. The sediment was compact, organic clay. Rootlets still persist. Gastropods were very small and less in quantity.

LITHOUNIT III - 60-130 cm - Dark brown, Homogenous, compact, with silken slit, thick black sticky clay. Shells absent. At the depth of -.110 cm $CaCO_3$ coated Manganese pellets were observed.

LITHOUNIT IV - 130-180 cm - well-sorted yellowish brown, sandy mud with occasional MnO2 concretions is predominant. Occasional gravel, and greyish clay lenses, lots of Manganese nodules were observed. Almost devoid of any organic matter, shells absent.

LITHOUNIT V - 180-210 cm- yellowish brown gravelly sand with Manganese Oxide, Iron concretions, Granite gneiss, Mica schist, vein quartz, aplite, and occasional large litho lasts were observed. Shells absent. Microliths were collected and these could have been rested into the deposits from surrounding late Pleistocene terrace. Overall straightygraphy of MNS-14 is studied. It has been observed that, The Lake is shallow lake. Overall stratigraphy is O.K. it is a shallow lake, at times drying.

LITHOUNIT I- Shallowest <100 years.

LITHOUNIT II –Roughly covers 200-300 years related to relatively lesser humid (semi arid?) Phase.

LITHOUNIT III – pre 400 years –early medieval with imprints of medieval warning it is wet phase.

LITHOUNIT IV –It may cover part of deep lake phase and early historic period.

Biogeochemical formations

Iron Manganese precipitation was noted in the form of Nodular and pellet formation in the Mansar Lacustral environment. There appears to be no simple relationship of both the components, though predominance of iron oxide indicates shallower lake than the predominance Manganese oxide phase. Preliminarily it was a very shallow lake with water column depth not more than a few meters. There was no true anaerobic environment. Probably this aspect of Iron and Manganese precipitation is related to biological aspect of the lake. Thus it is a Biogeo chemical problem, which needs further studies in future.

Evidences other than Pollen assemblage

Generally Litho unit III(60-130 cm) indicate higher depth of water in lake than Litho unit II(40-60cm). Litho unit I(0-40cm) is much shallower than Litho unit II and III. Presence of iron oxide nodules in unit II are observed in most of the trenches taken in the Mansar Lake. Predominance of iron oxide indicates shallower lake than the predominance of Manganese oxide precipitation phase.

Owing to presence of nearby Manganese mines and Manganese ore, the emphasis was not given on the precipitation of Manganese oxide in relation to the climatic fluctuations. Iron concretion on the other hand definitely indicates temporary drying of lake. CaCO3; coated Manganese pellets were observed at the depth of 110-115 cm, in Litho unit III, which indicate lacustral deep water phase in Mansar lake.

Presence of shells in Litho unit I (0-40 cm) and Absence of any sand layers in these trenches suggests that the lacustral sedimentation has taken place in a relatively deeper part of the lake. Iron oxide nodule development in unit II indicate post depositional drying or lowering of lake level prior to the deposition of unit I, which is observed in all trenches. Thus the hydrology of unit II and III is very different from unit I. along with the fossil pollen assemblage data, the results were re-affirmed with the help of evidences from the other areas like hydrology of the lake, geological observations with respect to chemical analysis of sediment

The following observation were made on the preservation of fossil pollen grains due to the formation of $CaCO_3$ and Manganese nodules, percent organic carbon, pH of sediment, some of the observations are as follows:

1. Pollen grains having high percentage of sporopollenin in their wall are preserved better (Families Fabaceae, Asteraceae, Amaranthaceae, Euphorbiaceae, Poaceae, Acanthaceae etc.) than the grains of families Rubiaceae, Capparaceae, Apocynaceae, Lamiaceae, Combretaceae, Verbenaceae though these families have occurred throughout the profile.

2. Spores of fungi are quantitatively poor.

3. The selective destruction of pollen fossil was more in the samples rich in clay, (23.65% in Litho unit II & III) though the total pollen count was good.

4. Though the total organic content of the sediment is relatively less (0.61%) the fossil pollen was preserved and amiable for recovery.

5. The pH of Mansar soil sample is acidic (6.33) the pollen could be recovered, by using improvised method of pollen recovery, from the highly minerogenic lacustral sediments of the Vidarbha region.

Local Tank irrigation and its effect on lake hydrology

It is a very common practice of water management in this sub humid region of central India, since early historic times. Probably dependence on this system was more during late medieval period due to increased demand of water during the so called relative dry climatic phase related to Little Ice Age(c.1400-1800 c.A.D.). Such dams constructed at quite high upstream in Pench river valley (Totaladoh tiger reserve and dam) have diminished the contribution of pollen brought from the sub-Humid zone to the pollen spectra recovered from semi- dry land down stream. Thus a comparison of recent sediments with older one from Mansar lake deposits down stream have revealed environmental changes, because in older deposits pollen transport had not been affected by upstream bunds and dams and might have brought more pollen influx indicating Humid to Sub-Humid environment which came from the intake area of Pench river , a tributary of Kanhan river in the study area.Another reason for the poor influx of palynomorphs in Mansar lake was probably the practice of pumping of lake water for agriculture,This might have caused frequent complete drying up of the perennial spring of local origin, and might have changed the recent pollen spectra by elimination of one of the palynomorph sources.

Meteorological Data

It is common experience that no two years have the same weather. Further one year of exceptional weather can run together to form more prolonged periods of abnormal conditions such as droughts. The proxy climatic indicators such as pollen based vegetation changes, cycles of stream erosion, or meteorological data with respect to.. Mean rain fall, Temperature variation, Percentage humidity etc. are important to alternative interpretation as we move forward into historical times. The Holocene environmental history consequently warns us not to expect climate to have been constant over the last few centuries. There is also question whether the global climate has been warming up, as a result of culturally induced rise in atmospheric CO_2 levels.

The data of temperature and rainfall revealed this fact that there is slight decrease in temperature and increase in average rainfall during last few years in the study area. Meteorological data of last hundred years (1933-2003) was collected and analyzed further to study the fluctuation in climatic parameters like temperature, rain fall, wind speed and humidity and to see if it can be helpful in appreciating ancient environmental dynamics. The results of which are presented here;

Meteorological data,- Temperature variation (1933-2003)

YEAR	MMAX	YEAR	MMAX	YEAR	MMAX
1933	32.8	1957	33.25	1981	32.6
1934	33.0	1958	33.74	1982	33.55
1935	33.0	1959	33.24	1983	33.5
1936	33.0	1960	33.27	1984	33.3
1937	32.5	1961	32.9	1985	33.54
1938	33.0	1962	32.9	1986	33.7
1939	33.5	1963	33.1	1987	33.57
1940	33.3	1964	33.85	1988	34.27
1941	34.5	1965	33.73	1989	33.94
1942	33.6	1966	34.49	1990	32.65
1943	32.6	1967	33.85	1991	33.82
1944	33	1968	32.9	1992	34.54
1945	33.35	1969	34.4	1993	33.54

1946	33.24	1970	33.18	1994	32.72
1947	33.3	1971	32.4	1995	33.09
1948	33.3	1972	33.85	1996	34.27
1949	33.2	1973	33.7	1997	33.02
1950	31	1974	33.5	1998	33.35
1951	33.6	1975	33.23	1999	33.46
1952	34.2	1976	33.99	2000	33.93
1953	34.2	1977	33.9	2001	
1954	33.5	1978	33.05	2002	34.66
1955	32.8	1979	33.88	2003	
1956	32.6	1980	34.31		

Meteorological data (Nagpur) variation in rainfall (1933-2003)

YEAR	TMRF	YEAR	TMRF	YEAR	TMRF	YEAR	TMRF
1933	160.9	1954	102.2	1975	134.8	1995	102.3
1934	81.0	1955	120.0	1976	88.5	1996	61.2
1935	95.0	1956	108.8	1977	78.9	1997	88.2
1936	135.0	1957	85.7	1978	94.2	1998	90.6
1937	141.5	1958	89.3	1979	108.9	1999	82.7
1938	125.0	1959	119.2	1980	101.0	2000	78.0
1939	117.0	1960	103.8	1981	107.0	2001	
1940	137.0	1961	124.9	1982	109.6	2002	80.3
1941	87.9	1962	104.8	1983	109.3	2003	100.64
1942	126.6	1963	77.7	1984	63.3		
1943	75.4	1964	87.6	1985	109.9		
1944	111.0	1965	84.8	1986	82.5		
1945	112.2	1966	87.0	1987	79.5		
1946	115.3	1967	92.0	1988	71.8		
1947	103.1	1968	80.2	1989	53.7		
1948	98.1	1969	74.4	1990	96.6		
1949	116.9	1970	126.1	1991	76.0		
1950	61.0	1971	92.9	1992	65.7		
1951	84.9	1972	50.5	1993	109.4		
1952	56.7	1973	102.1	1994	145.7		
1953	69.5	1974	81.1				

Meteorological data (Nagpur) – Temperature, rainfall, windspeed. Variation.

YEAR	MMAX	TMRF	MWS
1933	32.8	160.9	5.5
1934	33.0	81.0	7.2
1935	33.0	95.0	5.3
1936	33.0	135.0	6.8
1937	32.5	141.5	6.6
1938	33.0	125.0	4.8
1939	33.5	117.0	5.9
1940	33.0	137.0	6.3
1941	34.5	87.9	7.1
1942	33.5	126.6	6.9
1943	32.8	75.4	6.2
1944	33.0	111.0	6.5
1945	33.3	112.2	6.3
1946	33.2	115.3	6.2
1947	33.3	103.1	5.8
1948	33.3	98.1	8.0
1949	33.3	116.9	7.2
1950	31.1	61.0	6.9
1951	33.6	84.9	6.8
1952	34.2	56.7	7.5
1953	34.3	69.5	6.9
1954	33.8	102.2	9.7
1955	32.8	120.0	11.1

YEAR	MMAX	TMRF	MWS
1956	32.6	108.8	10.7
1957	33.3	85.7	9.8
1958	33.7	89.3	10.2
1959	33.3	119.2	9.5
1960	33.3	103.8	8.9
1961	32.9	124.9	10.6
1962	32.9	104.8	10.6
1963	33.2	77.7	10.2
1964	33.9	87.6	10.0
1965	34.1	84.8	10.2
1966	34.5	87.0	10.5
1967	33.9	92.0	9.9
1968	32.9	80.2	10.1
1969	34.4	74.4	9.8
1970	33.2	126.1	9.3
1971	32.4	92.9	9.3
1972	33.9	50.5	10.1
1973	33.7	102.1	10.5
1974	33.5	81.1	9.1
1975	33.2	134.8	9.7
YEAR	**MMAX**	**TMRF**	**MWS**
1976	34.0	88.5	8.8
1977	33.9	78.9	8.6
1978	33.1	94.2	9.3
1979	33.9	108.9	8.1
1980	34.3	101.0	8.7

1981	32.6	107.0	8.1
1982	33.6	109.6	8.5
1983	33.5	109.3	8.5
1984	33.3	63.3	8.3
1985	33.5	109.9	7.6
1986	33.7	82.5	7.2
1987	33.6	79.5	6.9
1988	34.3	71.8	6.1
1989	33.9	53.7	5.8
1990	32.7	96.6	7.5
1991	33.8	76.0	7.8
1992	34.5	65.7	7.2
1993	33.5	109.4	6.8
1994	32.7	145.7	7.4
1995	33.1	102.3	6.7
1996	34.3	61.2	7.1
1997	33.0	88.2	6.5
1998	33.4	90.6	5.4
1999	33.5	82.7	5.3
2000	33.9	78.0	4.9
2001	Data not available		
2002	34.7	80.3	4.8
2003	34.16	100.64	4.63

Table 5.13- Meteorological data (Nagpur) variation in maximum percentage humidity

YEAR	8:30	17:30	YEAR	8:30	17:30
1933	63	44	1969	57	41
1934	57	40	1970	62	47
1935	57	41	1971	62	48
1936	65	47	1972	56	41
1937	64	45	1973	58	44
1938	61	46	1974	56	41
1939	57	39	1975	59	44
1940	59	37	1976	59	39
1941	60	38	1977	60	41
1942	60	38	1978	63	46
1943	64	39	1979	54	44
1944	67	42	1980	57	42
1945	60	40	1981	62	44
1946	63	41	1982	65	45
1947	63	42	1983	59	42
1948	65	42	1984	59	44
1949	63	45	1985	59	44
1950	59	42	1986	62	45
1951	59	41	1987	62	46
1952	56	37	1988	61	47
1953	56	37	1989	57	43
1954	56	41	1990	65	49
1955	54	45	1991	59	42
1956	56	47	1992	55	40

1957	63	44	1993	60	45
1958	65	49	1994	63	46
1959	60	45	1995	64	47
1960	63	45	1996	58	43
1961	61	46	1997	63	50
YEAR	**8:30**	**17:30**	**YEAR**	**8:30**	**17:30**
1962	62	43	1998	69	51
1963	61	43	1999	65	50
1964	55	40	2000	59	46
1965	55	40	2001		
1966	54	39	2002	59	46
1967	61	46	2003	64	51
1968	61	45			

Statistical analysis

1.Correlation between Mean Maximum Temperature and total mean rainfall is- 0.4005 and is significant at 5% level of significance (L.O.S.).

(Teal = 3.55, Ttab = 1.96 D.F. = 66)

If mean maximum temperature increases then total mean rainfall decreases.

2) Correlation between mean wind speed and % Humidity at 8.30 a.m. is 0.3144 and is significant at 5% level of significance (L.O.S.).

(Teal = 2.69, Ttab = 1.96 D.F. = 66)

Increase in Mean Wind Speed causes decrease in % Humidity at 8.30 a.m.

3) Correlation between Mean Wind Speed and % Humidity at 17.30 p.m. is 0.00287 and is insignificant at 5% level of significance (L.O.S.)

(Teal = 0.0233, Ttab = 1.96 D.F. = 66)

Change in Mean Wind Speed does not affect % humidity at 17.30 p.m.

4) Correlation between % Humidity at 8.30 a.m. and % Humidity at 17.30 p.m. is 0.563466 and is significant at 5% level of significance (L.O.S.)

Increase in percentage humidity at 8.30 am causes increase in percentage humidity at 17.30 pm.

(Teal = 5.54, Ttab = 1.96 D.F. = 66)

Statistical Test: "t-test to test the significance of correlation coefficient"

$H_o: \rho = 0 \qquad Vs \qquad H_1: \rho \neq)$

$$Tcal = \frac{|r| \sqrt{n-2} \sim t(n-2)}{\sqrt{1-r^2}}$$

Decision Rule: if Tcal> 1.96 then observed correlation is significant at 5 % L.O.S. otherwise (Tcal <1.96) observed correlation is not significant at 5% L.O.S. These investigations smoothly lead us towards summarization and logical conclusions of the study. It has been elaborated in chapter VI, followed at the end by a joint Poster presentation given at the 2nd AOGS conference held in Singapore, June 2005.

6

Summary and General Conclusions

1.   First multidisciplinary effort in hot tropical inland semi-humid region of central India, involving Bio-geochemical disciplines for appreciating Holocene and especially late Holocene climatic episodes.

2.   Study of Human palaeoecology with reference to excavations at Historical site of Mansar (c.200 B.C.to 700 A.D. dates as per pers.com: A.K.Sharma.)

3.   Multidisciplinary approach- Study of Lithostratigraphy,Field sedimentology , pollen analysis, Non -pollen palynomorphs, Neoecology and phytogeography, study of invertebrate (shells), vertebrates remains, lacustral archaeological remains in form of in washed antiquities (Tools, potsherds, Terracotta beads), Local geomorphology, Mineral magnetism and Radiocarbon dating have been undertaken. However, archaeology is not the main focus of research.

4.   The Human palaeoecological approach at the lake site has been designed to provide Historic and Geo-phytological basis for appreciating development of extant biodiversity in the region.

5.   Maximum number of trenches (22) has been dug into the semi-live swamp of Mansar from March 2000-2004,to understand the hydrology and formation of the lake and I have participated in excavation of 22 trenches within and around the lake.

6.   The multidisciplinary approach with conventional radiocarbon dating and basic sedimentological features for appreciating nature of climatic change from semi-humid to semi-arid   vis –a -vis Man induced environmental modifications during late Holocene times have been attempted through this research.

Broad based conclusions

The increase in the temperature through the late Holocene, together with some minor fluctuation has been reconstructed. These changes roughly fit into the general trend of global climate (Robert, 1993) changes as it has been believed, but there still remains the discussion for more detailed feature of the climatic changes during late Holocene period in the Mansar (Nagpur) lake region. Some of the broad based conclusions drawn from the palaeovegetation reconstruction are:

Plant microfossils- Fossil Pollen analysis

1.   The pollen record is dominated by pollen of woody taxa through out, but a slight decline in upper 45 cm (Litho unit I)in the MNS-XIV trench. The size of the lake is such that the pollen record gave both local and regional signals and thus it can be inferred that forest has dominated the landscape for the interval represented by this sequence.

2.   Multidisciplinary palaeoclimatic study, thus tentatively suggest climatic shift from semi-arid/semi-humid to semi-arid/arid conditions and return to present dry Sub-humid climatic conditions during later part of late Holocene period.

3.   Poaceae and Fabaceae are abundant throughout the record. Apart from Fabaceae the main woody taxa present were Euphorbiaceae, Caesalpiniaceae, Rutaceae, Combretaceae, Rhamnaceae, Myrtaceae, Tiliaceae, Sapotaceae, Meliaceae, Anacardiaceae, Apocynaceae.

4.   The herbaceous taxa do make a major contribution to the pollen assemblage in the sediments. They were Cyperaceae, Poaceae, Asteraceae, Amaranthaceae, Chenopodiaceae, Capparaceae, Fabaceae,Convolvulaceae, Lamiaceae, Acanthaceae, Verbenaceae,Liliaceae, Nymphaeaceae,

5.   Other taxa, which are frequently present with low relative abundances. They are, Zingiberaceae, Cucurbitaceae, and Orchidaceae.

6.   Throughout the entire profile the pollen assemblage and consequent biome is comparable to contemporary semihumid, conditions represented by the pollen assemblages of tropical semi humid conditions followed by semi arid conditions. The exceptions are samples at upper level, where arboreal pollen sum is lesser than that of the middle layers, which indicates a slight thinning of the forest cover in this upper sample as compared to the rest of the profile.

7.   In the upper 45 cm the predominant occurrence of pollen of grasses, sedges, and spores of ferns were noted. This may be due to opening of the landscape, probably in response to human intervention and comparatively more humid conditions indicated by occurrence of spores of Marsilea ,Azolla spores in local water bodies. Singh (1971) considered Cyperaceae to indicate higher humidity. It was observed that, Cyperaceae in the study area are extremely variable in distribution preferably responding to the moist conditions to the regional climate. Because the occurrence of Cyperaceae is rather uniform in all the litho units of MNS-XIV. On the contrary, a good number of Cyperaceae species (16 species in adjescent forest reserved patches in monsoon season, have been collected in various moist conditions, from the study area.

8.   The palynological record indicates that for most of the interval represented, landscape which has been dominated by mixed semi humid, deciduous forest only in Litho unit III., and there are evidences of thinning of the forests from Litho unit II as indicated by the dominance of Acathanceae , Poaceae, herbaceous Fabaceae, Cyperaceae families.

9.   Predominantly in the last couple of centuries there are evidences for thinning of the forest as seen from Litho unit II and I. Intense agricultural activity is indicated from the written records as well as by occurrence of Poaceae and Chenopodiaceae pollen grains.

10.   It becomes clear from the meteorological data and Government Gazetteer of   Maharashtra State (Mahabale and Chaudhari1987). that there is increase in the rate of precipitation and percentage humidity. The observation goes hand in hand with the occurrence of pollen assemblages, which are typical indicator of humid environment. e.g.Hypoxidaceae, Zingiberaceae, Orchidaceae, , Liliaceae,

11.   Evidences other than pollen assemblage. - palaeoecological techniques-

12.   Mansar Lake being an inland small basin was a promising site for investigation.

13.   MNS-I trench was the deepest or central part of the lake, which is dried up.

14.   MNS-II represents the peripheral portion of the lake, which has been reflected in MNS-II profile. However, where depth of water is fluctuating.

15.   MNS-III was near to present standing water and show recent pedogenesis, below 1.5 m, we could get the original late Pleistocene stream deposit upon which later sedimentation took place. Thus laying trenches from the peripheral dried lake bottom to the present day central portion of the lake provided us a sequential history of sediment deposition as well as vegetation.

16.   Total 22 trenches were excavated systematically by my guide   Prof. Kajale to understand these aspects and I had the privilege to participate in the excavations and acquire first hand field experience of late Quaternary stratigraphy and various other complementary disciplines mentioned earlier.

The lithounit wise results can be stated as follows,

MNS – XIV profile

Due to paucity of radiocarbon dates, there are obvious constraints on chronology and precise time periodwise interpretation of pollen assemblages. 4 samples were taken from 210 cm MNS – XIV profile.

Litho unit I - (0-40 cm)- It is shallowest profile of the age less than a couple of centuries representing the sub modern and modern pollen assemblage. (Families like Amaranthaceae,Capparaceae, Sapotaceae, Fabaceae, Mimosae, Myrtaceae, Rhamnaceae, Apocynaceae, Rubiaceae, Convolvulaceae, Verbenaceae, Lythraceae, Scrophulariaceae, Acanthaceae, Asteraceae, Liliaceae, Cyperaceae, Poaceae, Nymphaeaceae, Fungi and Chara).

Litho unit II- (40-60cm)- It covers 200-300 years and represent the dry phase. Iron concretions along with poor pollen record perhaps indicate gradual desication of lake. Pollen count is very poor representing families Sapotaceae, Myrtaceae, Combretaceae, Poaceae .

Litho unit III (60-130cm)- It represents perhaps 400 years of early Medieval period presented in fossil pollen records .The presence of CaCO3 nodules at the depth of 110 cm in this lithounit is interesting. Families, Bignoniaceae, Hypoxidaceae, Poaceae, Cyperaceae, Chara, Maximum arboreal pollen count, Maximum species diversity were observed. Pollen count and preservation is good. It represents mixture of elements of local as well as regional flora.

Litho unit IV (180-210 cm)- It covers lower part of lake phase and Early Historic period. The total pollen count per slide is poor, so also the preservation of pollen and spores. This indicates the initial process of lake formation. (Only few Poaceae, Cyperaceae members were observed in lesser proportion.)

General remarks on Mansar lake stratigraphy

Stratigraphy as revealed in MNS-XIV trench clearly showed damming of a sandy channel belonging to late Pleistocene stream. It is during the transitional phase from fluvial to fluviolacustral that we got the evidence of megafossils. The overlying clay is greyish in colour with clay partings. On exposure fluvial sand got hardened.

Thus, the channel sand of perennial stream and the occasional storm floods may represent the earliest lake formation period for which there is an epigraphic evidence (Pers.comm: A.K. Sharma) If this is presumed, then the lacustral sequence though only 1 m thickness, might have represented late Holocene period.

•Litho unit III indicated higher depth of water column in lake than Litho unit II. Litho unit I is much shallower than Litho unit II and III. Presence of juvenile stages of various molluscan species such as Lymnaca, Gyraulus, Melania, Ballamya, and Thiara in unit I probably indicates limitations imposed by desiccating phase preventing their further growth. Presence of iron oxide nodules in unit II are observed in most of the trenches in semidried portion of the lake. This probably indicates rapid drying phase in the intermittently exposed lake surface. Occurrence of Manganese oxide precipitation (Litho unit II, 40-60 cm) is observed in relatively less proportion.

• Manganese mine activity in study area

Owing to presence of nearby Manganese mines and Manganese ore, manganese nodules may have been inwashed into the lake sediments. So the emphasis was not given on the precipitation of Manganese oxide as indicators of the climatic fluctuations

• Absence of any sand layers in Litho unit III suggests that the lacustral sedimentation has taken place in a relatively deeper part of the lake.

•Iron oxide nodule development in unit II indicate post depositional drying or lowering of lake level prior to the deposition of unit I, which is observed in all trenches. The pollen record is relatively poor.

•Thus the hydrological conditions of unit II and III are very different from unit I.

Along with the fossil pollen assemblage data, the results were viewed with the help of evidences from the other areas like stratigraphy, hydrology of the lake, sedimentological observations with respect to chemical analysis of sediment, formation of CaCO3 and Manganese nodules, % organic carbon, pH of sediment. Some of the observations are as follows:

1.Pollen grains having high percentage of sporopollenin their wall are better preserved (Families Fabaceae, Asteraceae, Amaranthaceae, Euphorbiaceae, Poaceae, Acanthaceae etc.) than the grains of families Capparaceae, Apocynaceae, Lamiaceae, Combretaceae, Verbenaceae though these families have occurred throughout the profile.(Bhattacharya et al 2006)

2.Spores of fungi are quantitatively less represented the reasons for which need to be studied The destruction of fossil pollen was more in the samples rich in clay, (23.65% in Litho unit II & III) though the total pollen count was good. The reason of destruction need to be further investigated by sedimentological and geochemical studies.

3.The total organic content of the sediment is relatively less (0.61%) the fossil pollen was preserved and amiable for recovery because of improvised method.

4.The pH of Mansar soil sample is acidic (6.33), and the pollen could be recovered, by using improvised method of pollen recovery(After Anupama ,K.), from the highly minerogenic lacustral sediment of Vidarbha region. (Bryant, 1978)

5.Reduction of water levels during non-monsoon months and especially February to May is a routine phenomenon.

6.The rhizhoconcretions could be the result of microbial activity towards the upper layers of the lake profile dominated by Nelumbo, Nymphaea species. The black Manganese nodules with CaCO3 encrustation are a complex phenomenon and probably due to inflow of CaCO3 from surrounding late Pleistocene deposits. Further geochemical work would be useful for detailed interpretations.

7.MNS-I is the deepest profile in the lake. Here the uniform brownish black clay deposition is more than sandy gravelly portion indicating deepest lacustral phase.

8.MNS-II represents shallow water phase and fluctuating hydrology. Indications of flash floods are seen. Clay part is less, but gravel, sand, litholclasts are more. It represent very short period of standing water. On the contrary the white nodules are indicators of a relatively dry phase, also result of high temperature, and rapid evaporation rate.etc.

9. MNS-III again shows brownish red compact clayey mud one meter deep. But organic matter is less. This indicates the ongoing process of clay, and organic /inorganic sediment deposition.The organic matter is autochthonous and recently deposited.
10. Due to uneven nature of of Pleistocene terrace the deposition of the sediment is also uneven and the center of the lake seems to have shifted from MNS-I to present standing water body, near MNS-III.

11. MNS-I was the first central deep water part of the original lake, which remain so for a long period of time. After this a prolonged dry phase was experienced which doesnot appear to have been recovered completely till to date as far as the water level is concerned.

CHRONOLOGICAL CORRELATION

The result of fossil pollen assemblages has been deduced especially from the MNS-14 profile at Mansar. The 14C date at the depth of 180 cm is 1870-1630 years BP.

From the foregoing discussion, vegetation development during last 2000 years B.P. took place under various controlling factors such as availability of water, Temperature fluctuations, predepositional topography etc . It has also been worked out that at times forests were established and there after declined in the arboreal extent in the upper phase of the profile. The biotic factor has been identified as the main reason for destruction of forest leading towards herb and grassland formation in the immediate past. An effort has been made to work out the history of vegetation. Palynostratigraphic correlation of Quaternary sedimentary sequence have been used to reconstruct vegetation characteristics and land use by man for pastoral and arable systems, which made it possible to translate all finer details of vegetation dynamics for the past 2000 years.B.P.

While analyzing the signatures of past vegetation from the past 2000 yrs old deposits, it was observed that the vegetation was not static, instead shifts in vegetation were brought about by climate-landscape and human dynamics. This is indicated by the pollen diagram plotted from Vidarbha region of varying climate, precipitation, human influence evidential from pollen diagram.

The dating results could have been very helpful to establish the time sequence of the profile MNS XIV and, to reconstruct the palaeoclimate and palaeoenvironment history of subtropical central India. However, in spite of all systematic excavations at Mansar, two 14C dates could be obtained, at 164 cm-3320-3000 yrs.B.P. And at 190 cm –1870-1630 yrs.B.P.The reversal of the 14C date in Mansar lake deposit ,can be understood by taking in to consideration bioturbation of lake mud and possibility of the deposition of allochthonus organic plant material in the deposit from surrounding forested area around the Mansar lake can not be overlooked. Thus, by taking into considerations the evidences from Geology, Geochemistry, palaeovegetation assemblages, and nature of sediment the lowermost 14C date was considered as the most valid date. Much work needs to be carried out along with AMS dating of sequential deposits in future.

Climate and human impact -Competitive exclusion by introduced tree species, causing unfavorable climatic change. The main factors operating concurrently are;

1.   Decline of forests, clearing land by way of felling the trees and natural as well as Man made fires.

2. Colonization of the bare land with exotic plants such as Eucalyptus, Acacias, Cassias etc. in recent years.

3.These factors are effectively operating and are chiefly controlled by Man.

4.The pernicious practice of felling trees and fire promote the formation of open herb- grass land formation. It has also been observed by palynological investigation that forest got transformed into shrub –Herb-Grass land with the advent of Man into landscape in Sub-modern period. This process was intensified and shrub landscape got converted into the herbaceous grass land (Fig.4.3). It may be suggested that the present day shrub -grass land type of vegetation can be designated as climatic climax of plant community at Mansar lake site and the forest as a sub-climax ,coupled with plantation of exotic trees.

Human ecological Changes in Historical time.

Palynostratigraphcal correlation of late Holocene sedimentary sequence have been used to reconstruct vegetation characteristics and land use by Man for pastoral and arable practices. This helped to get all finer details of vegetation dynamics for the past 2000 years.

Process of human induced deforestation are quite rapid and might have occurred in a short time, depending on how sensitive was the environment and what was the intensity of human activities.

The contribution made by Man to such process , however, have tilted the natural trends towards further deterioration of ecosystem.During preagricultural time, Man, who had to follow appropriate environments suitable for his needs of hunting and food gathering. Initiation of agriculture is a period of active intervention and encroachment on the environment. The early stage caused only minor changes in the close vicinity. With the introduction of plants and animals husbandry the unintentional development of weeds took place in natural environments. The pollen record is dominated by pollen of woody taxa through out, but a slight decline in upper 45-cm in Litho unit I of MNS-XIV profile. This pollen record is mainly regional signal and thus it can be inferred that forest has dominated the landscape during the time interval represented by stratigraphic sequence exposed in MNS-XIV profile.

The impact Land uses upon contemporary soil erosion

One of the most important practical legacies that Holocene researchers may have to offer through such research and data sets is in helping to formulate conservation policy in a world of rapidly changing global climate. Most conservation plans are essentially static, in that they do not accommodate future climate change. Setting aside nature to its own development protects a community or individual species. The boundaries of the reserve are fixed, but the community is not. As climate changes, it induces the species to migrate, and we may expect community turnover and local extinctions of a particular species. (Mackay et al 2003) Active management of small reserves may delay or even halt this process, however in larger areas a new conservation approach is needed. Identification of biodiversity hotspots and areas of significant threat are a first step toward protection. Understanding the resilience of communities to change and the probable response to change become major determinants of a successful conservation strategy. As the vast majority of global biodiversity is essentially tropical , there is an important role for Indian Palaeoecologist to play in this debate as well as formation of strategies for future adaptations.

The soil erosion and forest cover decline reconstructed from Mansar lake deposit suggests, change in the vegetation pattern and their distribution in late Holocene period. Human habitation, high rate of soil erosion, modern agricultural practices coupled with surface and subsurface Manganese and coal mining in the study area have lead further destruction in the ecosystem.e.g. The plant species like Dalbergia sissoo, which were abundant around Mansar lake area, have now become rare because of intensive mining activities and overexploitation.

DISCUSSION

Palaeopalynological study for reconstruction of past vegetation   can make significant contributions to environmental management. Pollen analysis can detect the impact of human activity on vegetation in sufficient details so as to relate historical events such as droughts, catastrophes and favorable climatic conditions. with their effects on vegetation

Pollen records from Mansar illustrated an essentially similar history of land use to those from archaeology and other documentary records. A pollen diagram from Mansar, which in many ways, serves to summarize the history of human impact on the vegetation during late Holocene, illustrates this. Mansar is a small inland lake, lying close to the foot hills, and yielded 210 cm thick deposit of pollen bearing sediment. As a result it contain a record of late Holocene ecological dynamics with a pollen assemblage divided in four litho units. Prior to 1630 yr. B.P. the vegetation comprises a initial fluctuating phase, followed by a stable semi humid woodland community with index taxa like family Anacardiaceae, Ebenaceae, Meliaceae, Euphorbiaceae, Rutaceae, Myrtaceae.

In view of the past and present features of the development of vegetation , it had been suggested that such pockets be considered as living fossil plants community which in due course of time may vanish and get displaced. Vishnu- Mittre and Gupta (1967,1971) expressed similar views while reconstructing the palaeoenvironment in Kashmir and Kumaon Himalaya region and Nilgiri (Tamilnadu)

Agriculture practices, animal browsing, disease and fire

Presence of charcoal indicates periodic burning of the landscape. Between Litho unit I and II (MNS-XIV, Sam.21, 60 cm).In Litho unit III

Semi humid taxa were abundant, mixed deciduous species were fluctuating and herbs grasses were sparse. This is what might be expected under a system of intensive irrigation based agriculture.

Thus human modification of woodland species composition is indicated by a decline in members of Ebenaceae, Meliaceae, Sapotaceae, Rubiaceae Combretaceae,Myrtaceae members.

Forest clearance associated with landscape use during late Historical period (Liho unit II) is clearly marked. There is a sharp increase in herbs and grasses, sedges and members of families such as Lamiaceae, Fabaceae, Amaranthaceae, Acanthaceae indicative of some sort of disturbed landscape associated with agricultural activity. There is periodic change in the balance between herb, shrubs, trees and the components of the landscape and the introduction of crops such as rice, pulses etc. These crops were already in existence in the study area by 1500 BC. as evidenced at the site at Adam in district Nagpur (Kajale 1994) In short, this pollen diagram records 2000 years of human cultural development under wild woods and of farming within secondary woodland, and late Historical period dominated by an agricultural landscape of fields and farms.

Effect of soil erosion on re-advancement of arboreal elements

The woodland clearance recorded at Mansar had permanent consequences on soil cover. The original black compact clays is preserved beneath the modern soil, however they are quite different from the soil, which now surrounds them. The fertile soil cover has been completely eroded to leave behind present calcareous soils. The eroded soil has been deposited down hills to form a colluvial deposit at the base of hill slope (Trench-MNS VII, MNS VXII, MNS XV). The unhealthy practice of felling trees and setting forest on fire due to ever increasing population pressure promote the formation of Shrub-Herb land. It has also been revealed by palynological investigation that forest got transformed into Shrub –Herb-Grass land with the intensive use of landscape during the last 2000 years. This process was intensified, and the shrub land got converted into the herb land. It may be suggested that the Shrub –Herb land should be designated as present climatic climax of degraded plant communities and the forest woodland as a sub climax phase prior to this. This is indicated in the pollen diagram of Mansar, in profile MNS-XIV, Lithiunit III (60-130 cm), showing maximum percentage of tree species and maximum biodiversity.

Climatic as well as anthropogenic factors had a marked effect on the stability of this environmental system, often reflected in a phase of accelerated erosion and sediment influx. It is thus necessary to study such degraded landscapes to learn palaeoecological lessons.The lake ecosystems are resilient in its recovery. They reflect the changes in the dynamics of surrounding ecosystem. The degradation of environment is mostly due to soil erosion. The soil conservation is vitally important for the maintenance of historical, ecological niches.

It is clear from the pollen record and other palaeoecological parameters employed at Mansar that it would be inadequate to talk of Human and natural causes of environmental degradation separately. Human impact is indicated by environmental degradations. Here several factors operate in combination. The factors like farming, fire, drought, pathogen outbreak with ever increasing population demands, might have been absorbed by the reducing tree species population, the combination of these factors had produced environmental stresses which could not be withstood or reverted. Human disturbance increased in this area, giving hardly any time for the biota to recover.

Environmental conservation, Management system and vegetation/ woodland management

The study area around the Mansar lake comprises pench river valley, pench tiger project, Tadoba – Andhari tiger project and reserved forest in Nagpur Chandrapur districts in Maharashtra. These forests may perhaps represent relicts of earlier undisturbed ecosystems. Thus the palaeoenvironmental studies in study area will help in understanding the trajectory, this reserve forest environmental system is following, and help us to manage ecosystem efficiently. It will further help in the identification and designation of ecosystem biotic factors particularly floristic elements, which have survived essentially undisturbed through the Holocene period because of protection offered by the Forest Department. This ancient woodland can retain genetic and other characteristics, absent in most disturbed areas of secondary woodland. Thus preservation of this gene pool is especially important since the policies, which are executed by the conversationalists, may not essentially be working for healthy maintenance of this ecosystem. Following examples have been observed to support this view,

Catastrophic pathogen outbreak, and anthropogenic disturbance.

Natural fire is long standing agent in this environmental management. Fire can mobilize mineral nutrients; regulate litter, accumulation of insect and other pathogens or parasites. However, the misguided fire suppression by forest managers in this area by fire line contours, has sometime serious adverse effects on forest ecology e.g. Decline of Shorea robusta by a stem borer insect parasite was observed in the adjoining regions of Nagpur in 1998-2000. What is more, this palaeoenvironmental research has shown that individual species have risen and fallen in relative abundance (examplified replacement of Shorea robusta with Tectona grandis) during last c 2000 years.

The present pattern of exploitation, e.g. reduced number of Diospyros melanoxylon Roxb. shows very few signs that, the lessons of environmental history have to be learnt and acted upon. This particular plant species is used for its leaves for beedi (local tobacco cigarette) preparation. So tender leaves are plucked, Branches are cut for development of fresh leaves, there are very less chances of flowering and fruiting, thus no fruit and seed formation takes place, leading to less percentage of seed germination and formation of new seedlings. Clear felling not only has pushed this area beyond the threshold of ecological stability, but also lead to severe soil erosion and hence made forest regeneration difficult or even impossible.

Thus, study of past environmental history and vegetation reconstruction in Nagpur area will offer some hope for the future management of ecosystems. Human induced forest clearance has so far been no less worse than naturally caused deforestation of earth, during Holocene the sub tropical as well as temperate forests were able to recover most of the area, but the span was thousand of years.

Pollen analysis has been instrumental in unfolding the fact that the semi humid   species are not regenerating under adverse conditions and therefore a phenomenal reduction in their aerial extent is recorded.Keeping in view wide spread herbaceous cover, one ought to think of future of the forest ecology. Ways and means are to be found to   spread natural woods into present herb land and overcome elements like Cassias & Eucalyptus or weeds like Prosopis and Lantana. Otherwise the continued exotic plantation and fast expanding grasslands clubbed with hunger for pastoral and arable lands will lead further forest destruction in this area.

Forest clearance phase –Modern time.

The study reveals that the vegetation in the surrounding areas of Mansar lake is far from being wholly natural and shows a particular distinctive pattern of land use, extensive mining activity (coal and Manganese ore) in the study area in addition to grazing and burning. The fuel problem is acute in this part of Vidarbha.It has been noted that high trees are burnt by making hole in the tree trunk and putting burning coal into it, so that the tree will die in few months due to internal combustion of vascular system. Poisoning the trees in reserve forests is also very common practice. Thus the idea of a primeval nature independent of Man, seems to be more functional and successful for the ecosystem functioning in the study area. The palaeoecological study in Nagpur has shown that humans have been an integral part of ecosystem and responsible for the changes in environmental and cultural history. (plate 6.1- 6.2)

Management system

For the restoration of forest ecology and proper management of the montanne environment, the first step to be taken is to reduce the biotic pressure & put a check on unplanned development. Ways and means have to be found to regenerate forest species in areas now covered by herbs , grasses and plantations. The slow but continuous process of plant succession has to pave the way for a thorough restitution of forest community which under the existing conditions is on the verge of extinction .

The data indicate quite clearly that favourable environments are typified by a greater variety and species number i. e. diversity of species, and have lesser dominance of certain taxa over the others. This in contrast to less favorable environments. As conditions become progressively adverse the tendency towards development of oligotropic or monotypic communities is much stronger e.g.Tectona grandis, Prosopis velutina, Butea monosperma, Ipomoea carnea, Nelumbo nucifera)

The use of fires by Man for clearing forests and preparing suitable areas for agriculture had also been practiced in the semiarid and semi humid regions for quite a long time. Reduction of arboreal pollen shares in the sediments and increased appearance of pollen produced by the weeds, or cultivated species, which occupy the cleared lands, has been observed in pollen diagram of Mansar. The decline in pollen produced by shrubs and trees was seen in the late Holocene period especially in Litho unit II.

Environmental conservation

The international Union for conservation of Nature and Natural Resources (ICUN) describes a National park as "One or several ecosystems not materially altered by human exploitation or occupation, and where the highest exploitation or occupation, and where the highest authority has taken steps to prevent or eliminate as soon as possible exploitation or occupation in the area "(ICUN, 1975).

The natural ecosystem is always dynamic and not stable. When viewed over the timescale of centuries, nature should not be made scapegoat in the name of modern science. If we look at the pressures of increasing population, urbanization and industrialization on ecosystem, particularly availability of land and removal of vegetation cover, or introduction of new exotic plant species as a package of afforestation, it becomes clear that the ecosystem is under tremendous threat.

While talking about the modern trends in Botanical or environmental research with respect to all the high technology subjects like Biotechnology or Bioinformatics one should not forget the importance of research in palaeoenvironmental studies. The comparative study of past and present vegetation will enable us to manage the ecosystem and environment. This is the issue of immediate concern in modern human society. The study has provided us with an overall view to estimate destruction of environment. The study of mega fossils, pollen records and other biological relicts have attempted discovery of the lost secrets of time, the pattern of change, adaptations and decline that have damaged ancient ecosystems. Habitat destruction, habitat fragmentation, overkill, invasive plant species associated with secondary effects have destroyed the past ecosystem. (Quammen 2000). Therefore, research models like this, projecting past, present and future species loss is going to be useful in future to restore the existing floral as well as faunal biodiversity. Thus the indigenous environmental knowledge, which is geographically specific, should be documented methodically. (Robert 1993)

The "best leave alone " on "habitat conservation" philosophy should be strongly adopted in the society, which is unaware of the future consequences. But can such research, provide us insight to wait that long? The success of the research lies, if we equip the society by all means to give only one   answer "Yes".

In summary the present case study holistically envisages multidisciplinary approaches from Neo-palynology, contemporary floristic, Quaternary pollen analysis, radiocarbon dating etc. with special reference to lacustral site of Mansar for unraveling palaeovegetational and palaeoecological conditions during the late Holocene period. It makes an humble effort to provide historical perspectives to the contemporary ecological problems, forest fluctuations and sustainable utilization of biodiversity prevailing in geographically central portion of India.

7

References

Agrawal, D. P. ,and Kusumagar,S.1967.14C dating with pollen analysis from sediments of salt lake and Bagirhat.Current.Science.36:566-568.

Agarwal, D.P. and Guzder, S. J. 1975. Quaternary studies on Western coast of India, preliminary observations. Palaeobotanist, 21:216-222.

Agrawal,D.P. 1987. Environmental changes in India during last 4 million years: Journal of the palaeontological society of India. 32: 1-4

Agrawal, D.P., & Kusumagar, S. 1967.14 C dating with pollen analysis from sediments of salt lake and Bagirhat. Current. Science. 36:566-568.

Agarwal, D. P., & Gupta,S.K., 1988. Climatic changes in India during the last 700,000 years . Proceedings of the IInd conference of the palaeoenvironment of East Asia from the mid tertiary

Agarwal,D.P. 1988.Palaeoclimatic data from Kashmir: A synthesis and some co-relations.Palaeoclimatic and Palaeoenvironmental change in Asia during the last four million years. Indian Science Academi, New Delhi. pp 1-10

Agrawal, D.P., Dodia, R., Kotlia, B .S., Razdan, H., & Sahni, A. 1989.Quaternary pollen analysis from deposits from Kerawas .Hirpur formation. Kashmir. Palaeogeography. Palaeoclimatology Palaeoecology. 73: 267-286.

Agrawal D.P., Khoshoo T. N., Sharma M. 1991. Indian Geosphere − Bioshpere programe some aspects. National academy of science India. Haranand publication. Vikas publishing house Pvt. Ltd. New Delhi.

Agarwal, D. P. 1995. Reconstructing the past climate and environment.

Almeida, M.R. (1996-2001), Flora of Maharashtra Vol. I-III, Orient press, Mumbai.

Almeida, M.R. Dutta, S. and Almeida, S.M. 2003. Glimpses of the phytogeography of Maharashtra, Journal Bombay Natural History society, 100 (2 & 3):. 559-582.

Anupama. K.,Ramesh B.R. and Bonnefille,R.Pollen analytical work in South India.2000.Review of Palaeobotany, Palynology.108:175- 196

Anupama. K, Taieb, M.P., Sutoa, J.P., and Prasad, S. 2000. Pollen analysis of modern surface samples and fossil cores in South India. Workshop on South Asian palaeoenvironment. Pune, India

Anupama K., Aravady, S., and Prasad, S. 2002. Pollen and ecological studies in the estern Ghats. A new methodological approach. National Science Congress, Eastern Ghats Tirupati, A.P.(Personal communication)

Badam, G. L., Sathe, V. G., and Ganjoo,R.K., 1983. New fossil discoveries from the Manjra valley, Central Godavari Basin.

Balapure, K.M.1966a. Some plant records from Chandrapur.Journal of Bombay Natural History Society.62:455-462.

Barbara,A.,Meher,and Thomson,R. 1999.Quaternary climate , environments and Magnetism, Cambridge univ Press. Cambridge L

Barboni. D., Bonnefille, R. 2001.Precipitation signal in pollen rain from tropical forests, South India. Review of palaeobotany and palynology114 : 239 –258

Barui, N .C., & Chanda, S. 1979 .1992.Palynological studies of peat profile from Metro-railway excavation at Culcutta. Proceedings of. Indian national Science Academy. B58 (4): 191-200.

Basavaiah, N and Khadkikar AS (2004) Environmental magnetism and it's application towards Palaeomonsoon reconstruction. The Journal of Indian Geophysical Union, 8 (3): 1-14.

Bates, C. D., Coxon, P., & Gibbard, P. L. 1978. A new method for the preparation of clay rich sediment samples for palynological investigations, New Phytologist 81: 455-465.

Behre, K.E. 1981. The interpretation of anthropogenic indicators in pollen diagrams, pollen and spores, 23: 225-45.

Bennet ,S.S.R (1966) .Name changes in flowering plants of India and adjacent Region.,Triseas publishers,94A, Indra Nagar Colony,Dehradun .

Berglund, B. E.1986. The Handbook of Holocene palaeoecology and palaeohydrology.

Bharadwaj, D.C. and Anand, Prakash. 1974. Palynostratigraphy of lower Gondwana Sediments from Umrer Quarry, Nagpur, Maharashtra, India. Geophytology, 4 (2): 130-134.

Bhatia, S.B., and Mannikeri, M.S. 1976 .Some Charophyta from the Deccan Inter trappean beds near Nagpur, Central India. Geophytology 6(1) : 75-81.

Bhattachrya, K.S.,Chanda, S.,and Bauri ,N.C.1986.Vegetational history and biostratigraphy of the late Quaternary sequence of Tinsukia ,Upper Assam,India.Bulletin of Geology, Mineral and Meteorologycal Society of India 54:202-207.

Bhattacharya, K., Chanda, S. 1988. Late Quaternary vegetational history, palaeoecology and Biostratigraphy of some deposits of Bramhaputra Basin, Upper Assam. India. Palaeoecology, vol; 23-24 : 225 – 237.

Bhattacharya,K.,Mujumdar,M.R.,Bhattacharya,S.G.2006.A Textbook of palynology,Basic and Applied, New central book agency (p)Ltd.81,Chintamoni Das lane, Kolkata.

Birks, H. J. B., & Hilary, H. Birks(1980) Quaternary Palaeoecology . Edward Arnold Pub. Ltd.,41 Bedford square,London .

Birks, H.J.B.,1986. Late Quaternary biotic changes in terrestrial and lacustrine environments with particular reference to North-west Europe. Handbook of Holocene palaeoecology and palaeohydrology ,Ed. Beiglund,B.E.,John Willy and Sons Ltd.

Blasco, F. 1971.Study of past vegetation of the Pykara valley and Parson, Ootacamund. Trav. Soc. Sci. Tech. Francais Pondicherry. X: 1-436.

Brook ,J.,and Shaw,G.1968.Chemical structure of the exine of pollen walls and a new function for carotenoids in nature. Nature,219:532-533.

Brook, J., (Ed). 1971.Some chemical and geochemical studies on sporopollenin,Academic Press,New York. pp.351-407.

Bryant,V.M.JR.1978. Palynology: A useful method for determining Palaeoenvironment ,The Texas Journal of Science,Vol XXX, No 1: 25-40.

Caratini,C., Thanikaimoni,G.,and Tissot,C.1980,Mangrooves of India: Palynological study and recent history of the vegetation.Proce.of the IV Inte. Palynological Confe.,Lucknow,vol.3 :49-59.

Caratini, C., Delibrias, G., & Rajagopalon, G. 1990. In: Jain K.P. and Tiwari, R.S. (Eds.),Palynological analysis of surface sample and profiles from Kalibanga ,Orrisa. Proceedings of. Symposium-. Vistas in Indian Palaeobotany. Palaeobotanist. 38: 370-378.

Champion, H. G. 1936. A preliminary survey of forest types of India and Burma. Indian forester record. silva. 1:286.

Chanda, S., & Mukherjee, B.B. 1969.Radiocarbon dating of two microfossiliferous Quaternary deposits in and around Culcutta ,Science & Culture. 35: 275.

Chanda, S. and Bhattacharya, K. 1987 . Quaternary pollen analysis in India with reference to vegetational history . Indian journal of Earth Science, sp. No. Modern Trends in Quaternary geology, 14: 283-295.

Chanda, Suniramal . 1973. Professor Gunnan Erdtman. Geophytology, 3 (1): 117 – 118.

Chauhan, M.S. 2004. Late Holocene vegetation and climatic changes in Eastern Madhya pradesh. Government of India Geology Magazine. V. 19(2): 165 – 175.

Cook,T.1901-1908.Flora of Presidency of Bombay- Vol I,II,III .,Taylor and Francis ,London,Reprt. Vol I-III,1958.

Cynar, L.C., Burden, E. Mc., Andrews, J. H. 1979. An inexpensive sieving method for concentrating pollen and spores from fine grained sediments. Canadian journal of earth science 16 : 1115 –1120.

D' Costa, M., & Mukherjee, B.B. 1986.Analysis of peat deposits of Lopchu and Barasenchal of Darjeeling hill,Phytomorphology. 36(1-2): 151-163.

Dan, Penny. (1999) Pollen grains in sands of time lake sediments contribute to the Archaeology of Thailand.- Expedition, 41. No. 3: 32-36.

Datta,N.P.1962.A rapid colorimetric procedure for the determination of organic carbon in soil; Journal of Indian Society. of soil science. 10:67-74.

David,R.H.,Thomas,K.D.1991.Modelling ecological change, perspective from Neoecology,Palaeoecology and Environmental Archaeology, Institute .of Archaeology,Univ college,London,31-34, Gordon Square, London,Wc1Hopy.

Davis, M.B. 1969. Palynology and environmental history during the Quaternary period, American. Scientist. 57: 317 – 32.

Day,P.R.1965.Practical fractionation and particle size analysis , methods of soil analysis-part I,Eds Black, Evans, White, Ensminger, and Clark, American Society.of agronomy, Inc. Madison, Wisconsin, U.S.A., pp 545-566.

De, Terra. H., & Paterson,T.T. 1939.Studies on the Ice age in India and associated human cultures. public. Carnegie. Institute. Washington 493: 1-354.

Dearing,J.1986.Core correlation and total sediment influx,in B.E. Bergland (ed.)Handbook of Holocene palaeoecology and palaeohydrology.Chichester:John Wiley, 247-272.

Deotare, B.C. 1995. Pollen recovery from minerogenic sediments. A Methodical approach, Man & Environment. XX(2) :101-105 .

Deotare, B.C. and Kajale M.D. 1996- Pollen analysis in Kuntasi : A Harappan Emporium on west cost. Man and environment, pp 291- 296.

Deotare,B.C.1996.Quaternary pollen analysis and palaeoenvironmental studies on the salt basins at Pachpadra and Thob, western Rajasthan,India,Priliminary observations, Man and Environment,V21:24-31.

Deotare, B.C. Kajale M.D., Kusumgar M.D., Sheela and Rajguru, S.N. 1999. Late Holocene environment and culture at Bari – Bavri, Western Rajasthan, India. Man and environment ,XXIV (I) .

Deotare, B.C. 2003. Recent finding in Purna basin of Vidarbha. Proceedings.of Joint Annual Conerence. Of ISPQS, IAS and IHCS, Venkateshwara Univ., Tirupati, pp9-10

Deotare,B.C.,Kajale,M.D.,Rajaguru,S.N.,Basavaiah N.2004.Late Quaternary geomorphology, palynology,and magnetic susceptibility of playas in western margin of the Indian Thar Desert.Indian Geophytology Union Vol8,No.1, pp .15-25.

Deotare, B.C.2006. Late Holocene climatic change :Archaeological evidence from the Purna basin, Maharashtra.Journal. of Geological Society of India,Vol 68: 517-526.

Dhavlikar, M.K.1999.Historical archaeology of India. Books and Books, New Delhi

Dhavlikar, M.K. 2001. Monsoon climate in the global perspective – I, Nile floods and Indian monsoon, Monsoon and Civilization, Proc. 2nd ALDP workshop, Pune, India ,PP 41.

Dimbleby, G.W., 1957.Pollen analysis of Terrestrial soils. New Phytologist 56(12):12.

Dimbleby, G. W. 1985. The Palynology of archaeological sites, Academic Press, London.

Dimbleby, G.W.,1978.Plants and Archaeology(2nd Ed),Granada, London.

District planning Map series-Nagpur- Maharashtra.National Atlas and thematic mapping organization.Department of Science and Technology.

Dodia, R., Agrawal, D.P. and Vora, A.B. 1984 Palaeopalynology Work in Kerawas,Kashmir. In: Whyte R.O. (Ed.) The Evolution of the East Asian Environment. 2: 569-573.

Dodia, R. 1988.Vegetation history of Kerawas, Kashmir. Proceedings of 2nd conference.on palaeoenvironnoent of East Asia from the mid-   Tertiary, Hong Kong. 1:680-691.

Dodson, J.R. 1983. Pollen recovery from organic lake clays : a comparison of two techniques, Pollen and spores, XXV (I) 131-138. Subdepartment of Quaternary Research, University of Cambridge, internal note.

Doyle,J.A.,1978,Origin of Angiosperms,Ann.Review. Ecology and Systematics 9: 365-392.

Edward,S.,Deevey,JR.1984.Stress,Strain and Stability of lacustrine ecosystem,Lake sediments and environmental istory,Eds.Elizabeth Y.,Haworth and John,W.G.,Lund-Leicester univ.press.

Eksambekar, S.P. 2002. "Contribution of the study of phytoliths to Bioarchaeology." Ph.D. thesis. Deccan College Post Graduate Research Institute Pune (unpublished)

Elsik, W. C.1966. Biological degradation of fossil pollen grains & spores- Micropaleontology 12:515-518

Erdtman,G.1945. Pollen morphology and plant Taxonomy .Svensk bot. tidskr.39.

Erdtman,G.1947. Suggestion for the classification of fossil and recent pollen grains and spores, Svensk. Bot. tidskr.41:104-114.

Erdtman,G .1952. Pollen Morphology and plant taxonomy.Angiosperms. (An introduction to palynology- I) Almqvist and Wicksell,Stockholm. Erdtman,G.1956. Pollen morphology and plant Taxonomy of Angiosperms. Hafner,New York.

Erdtman, G. 1969. Handbook of palynology: Morphology, Taxonomy,Ecology- An introduction to the study of pollen grains and spores.Hafman publ.Co. New York.

Evans,J.G.1972. Land Snails in Archaeology. London Seminar Press.

Faegri, K. and Iversen J. 1964. Textbook of pollen analysis. Munksgaard, Copenhagen.

Faegri, K., & Iversen ,J. 1975. Text book of Pollen Analysis. 3rd ed. Munksgaard, Copenhagen, Denmark, Blackwell scientific publication Ltd. Oxford, p. 295.

Fassett, N.C.1969.A manual of aquatic plants.The Univ.of Wisconsin Press, London.

Geel, B., Shinde, V., Yasuda, Y. 2001. Solar forcing of climate change and a monsoon related cultural shift in Western India around 800 cal. B.C. Monsoon and Civilization, proc. 2nd ALDP workshop Pune, PP. 35-39.

Ghosh, A.K. 1964.Lithochronology of Holocene Bengal basin. Indian Journal of Power- River valley Development Feb: 14-21.

Godwin, H.1957.Radiocarbon dating and post –glacial vegetation histry :Scaleby Moss.Proc.Royal Soc.London B.147:352-366.

Godwin,H.1960. History of weeds in Britain-The biology of weeds,pp 1- 10,Editor Harper,J.L.Blackwell, Oxford.

Godwin,H.1975,History of British Flora,(2nd Edn). Cambridge University Press ,Cambridge

Graham ,R.J.D.1911. List of wild plant found on the Nagpur and Telankheri farms,Nagpur.

Grichuk, V.P.1986.Application of palynology in the stratigraphy of Quaternary deposits of USSR.Review of .Palaeobotany and.Palynology.48 (4): 25-434.

Gupta, H.P. 1971.Palynological analysis of upper Pleistocene sediment of Cinnamara ,North Assam. Palaeobotanist 18:(3) 234-236.

Gupta, H.P. 1974. Aspect and Appraisal of Indian Palaeobotany. Palaeobotanist . 644-660.

Gupta, H.P. 1977.Pollen analysis of surface sample from Nainital Palaeobotanist 24(3): 215-244.

Gupta, H.P .1981.Palaeoenvironments during Holocene time in Bengal Basin ,India as reflected by palynostratigraphy, Palaeobotanist 27(2): 138-160.

Gupta, H.P. & Khandelwal A. 1982.Palynology of the Holocene sediments from Colara. Geophytology. 12(2): 313-321.

Gupta, H.P., & Sharma, C. 1982.Quaternary palynostratigraphy of India-A critical review .Palaeotological society. Of India. Special.publication.1:130-138.

Gupta, H.P., & Khandelwal, A. 1984. Proc.of Vth Indian geophytol. conf. Lucknow, 1983. Spl. Publ. The Palaeobotanical Society, Lucknow. 355-358.

Gupta, H.P., & Prasad, K. 1985.Analysis of surface sample from Colgrain, Ootacmund,Nilgiri. Journal of Palynology. 21:174-187.

Gupta,H.P., & Sharma, C. 1986.pollen flora of North-West Himalaya. Indian association of palynostratigraphars.Lucknow.

Gupta, H.P., & Khandelwal, A. 1990.Palynology of Holocene sediments from Kolara In: Jain, K.P. & Tiwari R.S (Eds.). Proceedings of. Symposium-. vistas in Indian Palaeobotany. Palaeobotanist. 38: 379-393.

Gupta, H.P., & Yadav, R.R. 1990.Palynological studies from Paradip and Jambu island, Orissa In: Jain, K.P. & Tiwari R.S. (Eds.) Proceedings of. Symposium- vistas in Indian Palaeobotany. Palaeobotanist. 38: 359-369.

Gupta, H., Sharma, Chhaya. 1992. Vegetational history and palaeoenvironment of Ningle Nallah, Lower karewa, Kashmir. Geophytology, 20 (2) : 103-105.

Gupta, H.P.1992.Changing pattern of vegetation in Kashmir valley Palaeobotanist. 40: 354-373

Gupta, S.K., 1988. Recent palaeoclimatic data from Indian region with reference to climatic modeling and environmental studies, Indian Nath. Sci. Acad. 54 A(81988): 343 –353.

Hait, A.K., Das, H.K., Ray, A.K., & Chanda, S. 1994b.Palynological studies of subsurface sample of Digha, South Bengal. Journal of Palynology. 30:73-78.

Handbook of Agriculture,1969.Indian Council of Agriculture Research, Govt. of India New Delhi.

Horowitz ,A.1992. Palynology of Arid land : Elsevier science publishers, Amsterdam, Netherland.

Hunt, C. O. 1955. Recent advances in pollen extraction techniques. Palaeobiological investigation. In N.R. J. Aelter, D.D. Bentson, G., Rahi N.C.A. 181-189.

Hunt, C.O. 1985. Recent advances in pollen extraction techniques : A Brief review. Palaeobiological Investigation, Edited by Aeller,N.R.J.,Bentson, G.,Rakib,N.C.A.,181-189, Dept of prehist and archaeology University of shettield, Shettield.

Huntington,E.1906. Pollen analysis of sediments Pangong lake, Ladakh,India.,Journal of .Geology.15:599.

Hyde,H.A.and Williams, D.A.1944. Use of Gravity slide to detect air spora.New Phytology.43:49-61.

Iversen, J. 1964. Plant indicators of climate , soil, & other factors during the Quaternary period. 1 .Ameri. Sci. , 57: 317-32.

ICUN (1975) World directory of National parks and other protected   areas. Morges, Switzerland

Jackson ,M. L . 1962. Soil chemical analysis , Asia publishing house . New Delhi.

Janssen, C.R. 1980. Where has all pollen gone? On the reconstruction of past vegetation by pollen analysis-A Review, Porceedings of. IVth International . palynology conference ,Lucknow, India. Jemett, G . and Own ,J.A.K. 1996. Review of palaeobotany, 64 (1990): 205- 211.

Joshi,R.V.,and Deotare,B.C.1983.Chemical analysis of Archaeological deposits from India. Deccan College Post Graduate Research Institute,Pune.

Joshi, J.P., And Sharma, A.K. 2000. Excavation at Mansar, Dist Nagpur (1994-95)-A review, Maharashtra. Bulltn. Of Indian archaeology soc. (30):56

Kajale, M.D., Badam, G.L., Rajguru, S.N. 1976. Late quaternary history of Ghod valley Maharashtra. Geophytology, 6 (1): 122-132.

Kajale, M.D. 1990 .Plant remains, in exavation at Kaothe (M.K. Dhavalikar, Vasand Shinde, and Shubhangana Atre eds), PP 265 – 280, Pune Deccan College.

Kajale, M.D. 1991. Current status of Indian palaeoethanobotany : introduced and indigenous food plants with a discussion on the historical and evolutionary development of Indian agriculture and agricultural system in general, in new light on early farming, recent developments in palaeoethanobotany, (Jane, M. Renfrew eds) PP-155-189, Edinburgh : Edinburgh University Press.

Kajale ,M.D.1994.Archaeological investigations on multicultural site at Adam, Maharashtra, with special reference to the devlopment of Tropical agriculture in parts of India. In:J.G. Hather (Ed.) Tropical Archaeobotany : Applications and New Development. Routledge.London,New York, pp 34-50.

Kajale, M.D., and Deotare, B.C.1995. Late Quaternary Palaeoenvironmental studies in western Rajasthan ,India .Part I: Initial observations and lithostratigraphy of salt Lake deposits in Indian desert margins.Bulletin of Egyptian Geographical Society,Tome LXVIII, 68:129-156 .

Kajale, M. D. 1996. Palaeobotanical investigations of Balathal : preliminary result. Man and environment. XXI (1)

Kajale, M. D. 1996 a. Plant remains, in Kuntasi : A Harappan emporium of West Coast (M.K. Dhavalikar, M.H. Raval and Y.M. Chitalwala eds) PP 285 – 289, Pune : Deccan College.

Kajale, M.D. 1996 b Palaeobotanical investigations at Balathal : Priliminary results. Man and environment. 21 : 98-102.

Kajale, M.D. 1996 d Plant resources and diet among the Mesolithic hunters and forgers. In colloquium 33. Bioarchaeology of Mesolithic India : An integrated approach. Vol. 16. The Prehist of Asia and oceania, 13th Inter. Congress prehist protoshit sciences, Forli (Itali) 8-14 Sep. 1996, Forli, pp 251-253.

Kajale, M.D. 1996 e. Neolithic plant economy in parts of lower Deccan and South India. Abstracts – The section of the 13th internet congress prehist protohist sciences, Forli (Italy) 8-14 Sept 1996. Forli, pp 67-70.

Kajale, M.D., and Deotare, B.C. 1997. Late Quaternary environmental studies on salt Lakes in Western Rajasthan, India : a summmarised view. Jourl. Of Quat. Sci. 12 (5): 405 –412

Kajale,M.D. 1997. Evidence of rice (Oryza sativa Linn) from Koppa: a megalithic site in Karnataka. Man and Envir. 22 : 97-101.

Kajale, M.D., Deotare, B.C., Rajguru, S.N. 2001. Palaeomonsoon and prehistoric cultures of the than desert. Northwest India. Monsoon and civilization, proc. 2nd ALDP workshop, Pune, India.

Kamble, S.Y.,Pradhan, S.G.1988. Flora of Akola District,Maharashtra,BSI Calcutta..

Kerney, M.P.1977. A proposed zonation scheme for late –glacial and post glacial deposits using land mollusca,Jour.of Archaeological Science,4:387-390.

Kitagawa,H., Nakagawa, T., Sasaki, K., Sawai,Y., Naruse,J., Van der Plicht., Yasuda, Y.2001. Deglacial record of Eastern Asia climate from annually laminated sediments of Lake Suigetsu, Japan, Monsoon and civilization, proc. 2nd ALDP workshop, Pune, India.

Kotlia, B.S., and Jaishri, Sanwal. 2004. Fauna and palaeoenvironment of late quaternary fluviolacustral basin in central kumaon Himalaya. Current science. Vol. 87(9-10) :1295-1299.

Krishnamurty,R.V., Aggrawal, D.P.,Misra, V.N.and Rajaguru,S.N.1981. Palaeoclimatic influence from behavior of radio-carbon dates of carbonates from sand dunes of Rajasthan. Proceedings of the Indian Academy of Science ,(Earth Planet Science),90:155-160.

Kroll, H. 1996-97. Literature on archaeological remains of cultivated plants, Vegt. Hist. Archaeobot . 7: 23-56.

Kshirsagar, A., and Badam, G. L. 1990. Biochronology and fluorine analysis of some pleiostocene fossils from central & western India. Bulletin DCPRI. 49: 199-211.

Kshirsagar, A., & Gogte, V. D. 1990. Fluorine determination in Archaeological bones by Ion selective electrode. Bulletin DCPRI. 49: 213-216.

Kshirsagar, A. 1993. Role of Fluorine in the chronometric dating of Indian stone age culture. Man & Environment XVIII (2) : 23-32.

Kumaran, K.P. N., Limaye, R.B. Rajshekhar, C and Rajagopalan, G.2001. Palynoflora and radiocarbon dates of Holocene deposits of Dhampur, Sindhudurg district, Maharashtra, Current science, 80: 1331-1336.

Kumaran, KPN, Shindikar MR and Limaye RB (2004a) Mangrove associated lignite beds of Malvan, Konkan: evidence for higher sea level stand during the Late Tertiary (Neogene) along west cost of India. Current Science, 86(2): 335-340.

Kumaran, KPN, Shindikar MR and Limaye RB (2004b) Fossil record of marine manglicolous fungi from Konkan, India. Indian Journal of Marine Sciences, 33(3): 257-261.

Kumaran, K. P.N., Nair, K.M. Shindikar, M. Limaye, R.B. and Padamala, D. 2005, stratigraphical and palynological appraisal of late quaternary mangrore deposits of the west coast of India, Quaternary Res. 64: 418-431.

Lamb, H. M. 1977. Climate : Present, Past, and Future, Metheum and Co. , London, Vol. I & II .

Lamb, H. M. 1984.Modern pollen spectra from Labrador and their use in reconstructing Holocene vegetational history,Jour.Ecology, 72:37-59.

Lee,J.D.1995.Concise in Inorganic Chemistry Chapman and Hall,Oxford University press,London.pp 410-411

Lentfer, C. J., and Boyd, W.E. 1997 An assessment of techniques for the deflocculation and removal of clays from sediments used in Phytolith analysis. Journal of Archaeological. Science. 26:31-44.

Lentfer, C. J., and Boyd, W.E. 2000. Simultaneous extraction of phytotiths pollen and spores from sediments. Journal of Archaeological. Science , 27: 263-372.

Limaye, R.B. 2004. Contirbution to palaeopalynology of the coastal deposits of Maharashtra. India Ph.D. thesis, University of Pune.

Limaye, R.B., Kumaran, K.P.N. Nair, K.M. and Padmala, D. 2007. Non Pollen palynomorphs as potential palaeoenivornmental indicators in the late Quaternary sediments of the West coast of India. Current science, Vol. 921(10): 1370-1382.

Lozek,V.1986. Mollusca analysis,in B.E.Bergland (Ed.) Handbook of Holocene palaeoecology and palaeohydrology.,729-740. Chichester: J. Wiley

Mahabale,T.S.1966. Flora of Deccan:Past and Present. Proce.53rd Indian National Science .Congress.Chandhigarh,Botany section,:1-30.

Mahabale,T.S.,Chaudhari,K.K.1987.Maharashtra State Gazetteers, Govt. of Maharashtra, General state series, Botany part IV, Botany and Flora of Maharashtra, ,Gazetteers Dept., Govt. of Maharashtra, Bombay.

Mahajan, D. R., and Mahabale, T.S. 1973. Quaternary flora of Maharashtra – 1, The pravra river basin, Dist. Ahmednagar, Maharashtra. Geophytology, 2 (2) :175 – 177.

Mackay,A.,Battarbee,R.,Birk,J.,Oldfield,F.(Eds) 2003.Global change in the Holocene Arnold publishers,Great Britain.

Malhotra, S.K., and Moorthy ,S.1971. Material for the Flora of Chandrapur District, Maharashtra State. Bulletin of Botanical Survey of .India.13: 292-311.

Malhotra ,S.K.,and Moorthy1992.A floristic account of Tadoba National Park and its Environs, Chandrapur District, Maharashtra State, Botanical Survey of India,Flora of India ,Series 4.

Mandal, J., and Kumar, Madhav. 2000. Stratigraphic significance of some Angiosperm pollen from Tinali oil field, uppar Assam, India. Palacobotanist, 49 (2): 197-207.

Mathew,K.M.1981.Illustration on the flora of Tamilnadu Carnatic .,Part I,II,III.,The Rapinat Herbarium, St.Joseph's College, Tiruchirapalli.

Meher – Homji, V.M. 1994. Climate changes over space and time : their representation repercussions on the flora and vegetation. Palaeobotanist .42 (2) : 225- 240.

Mirashi, M.V.1954. Studies in the Hydrophytes of Nagpur, Journal of Indian Botanical Society. 33: 299-308.

Misra, S., Ghate, S., Deo, S., Rajguru. S., Naik, S. 2001. Holocene climatic changes and response of human societies. Monsoon and civilization, Proc. 2nd ALDP workshop. Pune, India. pp 120- 121.

Moore, P.D., & Webb, J.A. 1978. An illustrated guide to pollen analyses. Hodder and Stoughton, London.

Moore, P. J., Webb , and Collinson,M. 1991. Pollen analysis IInd Edn. Blackwell scientific publication. Boston.

Mukharjee ,B.B. 1972.Construction of Pollen diagram from sediments of salt Lake, Baidyabati,Belgachia and Bagirhat, Eastern India,In: Ghosh, A.K..,et al .(Eds),Proceedings of Seminar on Palaeopalynology ofIndian Stratigraphy.Calcutta.1971:357-374.

Muller,J.1984.Significance of fossil pollen for angiosperms history, Annals of Missouri Botanical Garden 71:419-443.

Naik, V.N. 1998. Flora of Marathwada Vol. I- III. Amrut prakashan, Aurangabad.

Nair, P.K.K. 1960.Palynological investigations of the Quaternary (Karewa) of Kashmir .Journal of Science and Industrial Research. Delhi. 19C(6): 145-154.

Nair, P.K.K. 1962. Pollen grains of Indian plants, Bull. Nat. Bot. gardens, 52 : 1-35.

Nair, P.K.K.,Ed. Advances in pollen-spore research-4, Today and tomorrows printers and publishers.,New Delhi

Nath, Amerendra. 1989-90. Archaeology of Wardha Wainganaga divide. Archaeological Survey of India. Nagpur.

Nayar,T.S.1984.The systematic palynology of angiosperms in Maharashtra state. Ph. D. Dissertation. Sardar Patel University, Vallabh Vidyanagar, Gujrat. (unpublished).

Nayar,T.S.1990.Pollen flora of Maharashtra state,India. Scholarly publication, Today and Tomorrow printers and publishers,New Delhi.

Patel,R.L.1968 Forest flora of Melghat,published by Bishan Singh and Mahendra Pal Singh,Dehra Dun.

Piper,C.S.1966. Soil and plant analysis,Hans publishers,Bombay.

Possehl, G. H. 2001. Monsoon and south Asian history, Monsoon and civilization,force 2nd ALDP workshop. Pune. India. PP 30-31.

Prakash V. 1973. Palaeoenvironmental analysis of Indian tertiary floras. Geophytology,2(2) : 178 – 201.

Prasad, S. and Anupama, K. 2006 Light microscopic studies on pollen grain of selected cyperaceae species from Southern Tamil Nadu. Revelance in Late Holocene sediment studies (In press). French Institute of Pondicherry, Pondicherry, India.

Quammen ,David.2000.Planet of weeds-Tallying the losses of Earth's animals and plants.Span,September: 18-58

Raghubanshi, A.S., Singh, J.S., and Venkatchala, B.S.1991. Environmental change and biological diversity: present past and future. Palacobotanist. 39 (1): 86-109.

Rajguru S. N. 1973. Late Pleistocene climatic changes in western India, in Agrawal & Ghosh (ed), pp80-87.

Rajshekhar, C. Gawali, P.B. Mudgal, T.R. Reddy, P.P. and Basavaiah, N. 2004 Micropaleontology and mineral magnetic evidences of the Holocene mudflats of navalkhi , gult of kuchch, J. Inidan geophys, Union, 8, 71-77.

Ramkrishnan, P.S. 2003. Global change natural resource management and sustainable development. Tropical ecology. 44 (1) : 1-6.

Rao, A.R., & Menon, V.K .1969.Analysis of nonpolliniferous remains from Pykara sediments. Journal of Palynology. 5:74-84.

Rao,K.P.,and Ramanujam,C.G.K.1982.Palynology of Quilon beds of Kerala state,South India-2:Pollen of Dicotyledons and discussion,Palaeobotanist,30:68-100.

Ratan, R., and Chandra,A. 1983. Palynological investigations of the Arabian sea: Pollen / spores from the recent sediments of the Gulf of Kachchh, ,India . Palaeobotanist. 31:165-175.

Ratan, R., & Chandra, A. 1984.Palynological investigations of the Arabian sea: Pollen and spores from the recent sediments of the continental shelf off, Bombay ,India . Palaeobotanist 31:218-233.

Robert, Neil.1993. The Holocene-An environmental history,Blackwell Publishers,Oxford.

Robin, L. C. 1984. Effects of charcoal on pollen preparation procedure. Pollen et spores. XXVI- No. 3-4: 559-576.

Roy, P., and Chanda, S. 1988.Analysis of the late Quaternary deposits near Loktak lake,Manipur. Transactions of Bose Research Institute 51(3): 73-80.

Saad, S. I.1974.Palynological results and their bearing on the theory of continental displacement, pp 70-77,Advances in pollen- spore research-1,Ed. Nair,P.K.K.,Today and Tomorrow 's printers and Publishers,New Delhi.

Sadashivan, T.S. 1988. Why basic science. Palaeobotanist, 37 (1): 134 – 141.

Santapau, H. (1967) Flora of Khandala 3rd Edn. Botanical Survey of India. Culcultta.

Santapau,H.1967.The flora of Khandala .Records of Botanical Servey Of India,Vol XVI:1.,3rd Edn.,The Manager of publication ,civil lines,Delhi.Govt of India.

Sarkar, S., Sengupta, S., & Chanda, S. 1984.Palynological analysis of the late Quaternary peat bog The East Asian Tertiary/Quaternary Newsl. Hongkong. 1:37.

Schade , J.D., Spon seller, R., Colling, S.L., stiles, A. 2003. The influence of Prospis canopies of understorey vegetation : Effect of landscape position. Jour. Of vege. Sci. 14 : 743 – 750.

Sengupta, S. 1966.Geochronological sequence of Bengal basin from Pleistocene to recent time. Bulletin of American Association of Petroleum Geologist. 50:1001-1017.

Sharma, C., and Gupta, H.P. 1984. In: Current Trends in Geology (Agrawal et al. eds.) vol. VI (Climate and Geology of Kashmir). Today & Tomorrow's Printers and Publishers, New Delhi:pp 91-95.

Sharma, Chhaya. 1985. On the late quaternary vegetational history in Himachal Geophytology, 15 (2) : 206 –218.

Sharma, Chhayya., and Chauhan, M.S.1988. Palaeoenvironmental inferences from the Quaternary palaeostratigraphy of Himachal pradesh and Kumaon ,India. Proceedings of .Indian National Academy of Science.Vol 54A (3):510-523.

Sharma, C. 1992.Comparative pollen diagrams of Himachal pradesh showing fluctuation in Holocene period. Palaeobotanist. 40:374-382.

Sharma, Chhaya., Chauhan, M.S., Rajgopalan, G. 2000. Vegetation and climate in Gharwa Himalaya during last 4000 years. Palaeobotanist, 49 (3): 501-507.

Sharma, Chhaya .2001. Modern pollen rain compared vegetation in the Himalayas. Palaeobotanist foundation, Proceedings of IX. Inte. Palynological Cong. Hauston, Texas USA P. 557-565.

Sharma, Chhaya. 2001. Palynostratigraphy of Himalayan lacustrine sediments. In Goodman, D.K. and Clarke, R.R. (eds.) Proce. of IX Inte. Palynological Cong. Houston, Texas, USA 1996. American association of strategic palynologists foundation pp. 527-532.

Sharma, Chhaya., Shrivastav, C., Yadav, D.N. 2003. Holocene history of vegetation and climate of fresh water puntota (Degana) .BSIP, Lucknow, India.

Sharma,B.D.,Karthikeyan,S.,Singh,N.P.(Eds).1996.Flora of Maharashtra state-Monocotyledons Flora of India ,series2.Botanical Survey of India.

Shaw, J. 1971. The chemistry of sporopollenin: Sporopollenin (Eds. J. Brooks et al. Academic press.

Shindikar, M.R., Limaye, R.B., Kumaran, K.P.N., and Gunale, V.R. (2004) Past and present mangrove flora along Konkan, West Coast, India. Proceedings- of National seminar on 'New frontiers in Plant Taxonomy and Biodiversity Conservation' Thiruvanathpuram, India. 46

Singh, G., Joshi, R.D., Chopra, S.K., and Singh, A. B. 1974. Quaternary history of vegetation and climate of Rajasthan desert, India, Philosophical transaction of the Royal society of London, Series B. pp 267-467-501.

Singh. G., and Raymahashay,R. 2000. Salinity model inferred from two shallow cores at Sambhar salt lake ,Rajasthan; Jour.of Geological Society of India,56: 213-217.

Singh,G.1971,The Indus Valley Culture: seen in context of post –glacial climate and ecological studies in North-west India.Archaeology and Physical Anthropologyin Oceania,6(2):177-189.

Singh,H.,1988,Histry of aridland vegetation and climate –A global perspective

Singh, N. P., Karthikeyan, S.2000.Flora of Maharashtra State, Dicotyledons -Volume-I, Flora of India, Series 2,Botanical survey of India. Calcutta

Singh, N. P., Lakshminarasimhan, P., Karthikeyan, S., and Prasanna, P. V. (Eds).2001.Flora of Maharashtra state-Dicotyledons-Volume-2,Flora of India, Series 2,Botanical survey of India. Calcutta

Soni, Prafulla. 2003. Climate change and Restoration of tropical forests. Ecology and environment division. Forests Research Institute, Dehra Dun.

Stanley, D.J., and Hait, A. 2000.Holocene deltaic and underlying trangressive units in the western Ganga-Bramhaputra delta. Journal of Coastal Research. 16(1): 26-39.

Tara, S.V., Nakagawa, P.E., Gotanda,T.K.,Yasud, Y. 2001. How well can we reconstruct climate from pollen data in the area with complex topography and vegetation. Monsoon and civilization, Proceedings of IInd ALDP workshop, Pune, India, pp 140-141.

Thanikaimoni,G.1986.Fifth bibliography index to the pollen morphology of angiosperms.French insti.of Pondicherry,India.

Tissot ,C.1990.In: Jain KP & Tiwari, R.S. (Eds.). Proc. Symp. Vistas in Indian Palaeobotany. Palaeobotanist. 38: 348-358.

Tissot, C. 1987.Palynological analysis of two profiles from cauveri delta. Marine biological Association of. India. 29:16-22.

Tissot,C.,Chikhi,H.,Nayar,T.S.1994.Pollen of wet evergreen forests of the Western Ghats,India; Tropical Botanic Garden and Research Institute, Thiruvananthapuram ,and IFP Pondicherry Publication.

Tiwari, R.S. 1975. The first Indian geophytological conference vol. VI and VII .Geophytology vol. VI and VII, 5 (2) : 231 – 232.

Tiwari, R.S. 1993. A tretise on the potential of palynology in high caliber correlation and dating of calebrating Gondwana Sequence of India. BSIP. Lucknow India.

Traverse, A. 1988 Palaeopalynology, Unwin Hyman, London.

Tripathy. 1967. The Pleistocene alluvial deposits around Nevasa, Ahmednagar district., Maharashtra. Records of Geological.Survey of India.I. 95(2): 355-366.

Ugemuge, N.P.1986. Flora of Nagpur District, Sree Prakashan, Nagpur

Van Campo, E. 1983. Paleoclimatologie des bordures do la mer d' Arabic depuis 150,000 ans. Analyse Pollinique et Stratigraphie isotopique. these Montpellier.

Van Geel B. 2001 Non pollen palynomorphs. In tracking environmental change using Lake sediments, Terrestrial, Algal and siliceous indicators (Eds. Smol, J. P. et. al) Kluwer, Dordrecht, Netherlands Vol. 3: 99-119.

Van Geel, B. The palaeoenvironmental indicator value of non pollen palynomorphs in lake sediments, peat deposits and archaeological sites. Pollen, 2004 14, 276-277.

Van, Zeist W.1955.Pollen analytical investigations in the Northern Netherland with special reference to Archaeology,North Holland publishing company, Amsterdam.

Vaughn, M., Bryant, T .R. 1978 .Palynology -A useful method for determining palaco environment, The texas journal of science, XXX- No.1: 1978.

Vaughn, M.Jr., Bryant, JR., Richard G. 1983. The role of palynology in Archaeology. Academic press, India.Vegetation history and Archaeobotany, Vol 6(1),

Venkatachala B.S.1986. Palaeobotany in India – Quo vadis. Geophytology. 16 (1) : 1-24.

Venkatchala, B.S., Bande, M.B., Hari, K. 1988. Past of the present. Geophytology, 18 No.1 : 47-52.

Vidal , G. 1998. A palynological preparation method, Palynology, 12 : 215-220.

Vishnu-Mittre. 1964.Pliocene and Pleistocene boundry of vegetation in Kashmir valley by pollen analysis. Palaeobotanist. 12:270-276.

Vishnu-Mittre. 1966. Kaudinyapur plant economy in protohistoric and historic times. Palaeobotanist. 15:157-175.

Vishnu-Mittre,.Gupta ,H.P., and Robert, R.D. 1967 .Study of Late- Quaternary Lake deposits from Kumaon Himalaya, Current Science,36(2):539-540

Vishnu-Mitre., & Gupta, H.P. 1971.The origin of shola forest in the nilgiries,South India ,Palaeobotanist.(22):72-77.

Vishnu-Mittre., & Robert, R.D. 1971.Comparitive analysis of mega and microfossils from the lower karewa sediment ,Kashmir. Geophytology I: 84-96.

Vishnu-Mittre. 1972.Validity of the occurrence if Quercus and Alnus during post glacial period in Kashmir valley. Proc. Sem. Palaeopalynology Indian Stratigr. Calcutta: 348-358.

Vishnu-Mittre.,&Gupta,H.P.1972.Reconstruction of palaeovegetation of mid Holocene sediment from Sankrail and Jangalpur. Palaeobotanist 19(3): 297-306.

Vishnu-Mittre., & Guzder, S. 1975.The early domastication of plants in South and South East Asia –A critical review. Palaeobotanist 22:111-117.

Vishnu – Mittre., & Gupta, H. F. 1976. Pollen analysis of fossil soils along the bank of Ghod river , Inamgaon, Maharashtra. The Palaeobotanist , 23: 72-77.

Vishnu, Mittrre 1978. India- botanical perspective of quaternary. Jour. Of BSIP, 53 Univ. road Lucknow-226007.Moor, P. D., and Webb ,J.A. 1978. An illustrated guide to pollen analysis. New York

Vishnu- Mittre.1979.Early man in North-West India:Palaeobotanical evidence. Allied publishers,New Delhi.

Vishnu-Mittre.,& Sharma, C. 1979.Palynological analysis of Holocene deposits from the Nal lake, Ahmedabad.India Palaeobotanist, 26:95-104

Vishnu-Mittre .1981. Botanical perspective on the Quaternary. The Palaeobotanist ,28 & 29: 402-412.

Vishnu- Mittre.1982. Harappan civilization and the need of new approach.pp 31-38, In Harappan civilization–A contemporary perspective,(editor Possehl, G.L.),Oxford and IBH publishing company., New Delhi.

Vishnu-Mittre and Sharma, C.1984,Vegetation and Climate during the last glaciation in the Kathmandu valley,Nepal,Pollen et Spore,25:69-94

Von Post, L.1916 . Forest tree pollen in south Swedish peat bog deposits (Translation by Davis M.B. and Faegri K. 1967) Pollen et Spores.9(3):375.

Wadia, D. N. 1960. The post glacial dessication of central Asia . Monogr. Nat. Inst. Sci. India ,19-25

Wasson,R.J.,Rajguru,S.N.,Misra,V.N.,Agrawal,D.P.,Dhir,R.P.,Singhvi,A.K   and   Kameshwara ,R.1983.Geomorphology,late Quaternary Stratigraphy and Palaeoclimatology of the Thar dunefield;Zeitschrcift Geomorphologie N F Suppl. 45:117-151.

Webb, T. 1968 .Is the vegetation in equilibrium with climate. How to interpret lake quaternary pollen data, Vegetation, (67):75-91.

Webb, T. 1985. Holocene palynology and climate, A.D. Hecht (ed) Palaeo climate analysis and modeling chechester : John wiley. pp163-195.

Williams, M. A.J.and Clark, M. F. 1984. Late Quaternary environment in North central India. Nature . (London) 308: 633-635.

Wodehouse, R. P.1935. Pollen grains- Their structure, Identification , and Significance.,Science & Medicine.Mc Graw Hill Book Co , Newyork & London

Wodehouse, R.P. 1935 Pollen grains structure, identification and significance in science and medicine. Hafner publ. Co. New York.

Wodehouse, R.P. 1959. Pollen Grains,There structure , identification, and significance in science and medicine, Hafner Publishing Co, New York.

Yadav, S.R. and Sardesai, M.M.2002 .Flora of Kolhapur District,Shivaji University, Kolhapur.

Yasuda,Y.,Shinde,V.,Eds.2001. Monsoon and Civilization. The 2nd vol. International workshop of Asian Lake Drilling Programme.(ALDP).Pune, India.

Yasuda,Y.,Shinde,V.2004.Monsoon and civilization, Lustre Press,Roli books, M75,Greater Kailash II market, New Delhi.

PLATES

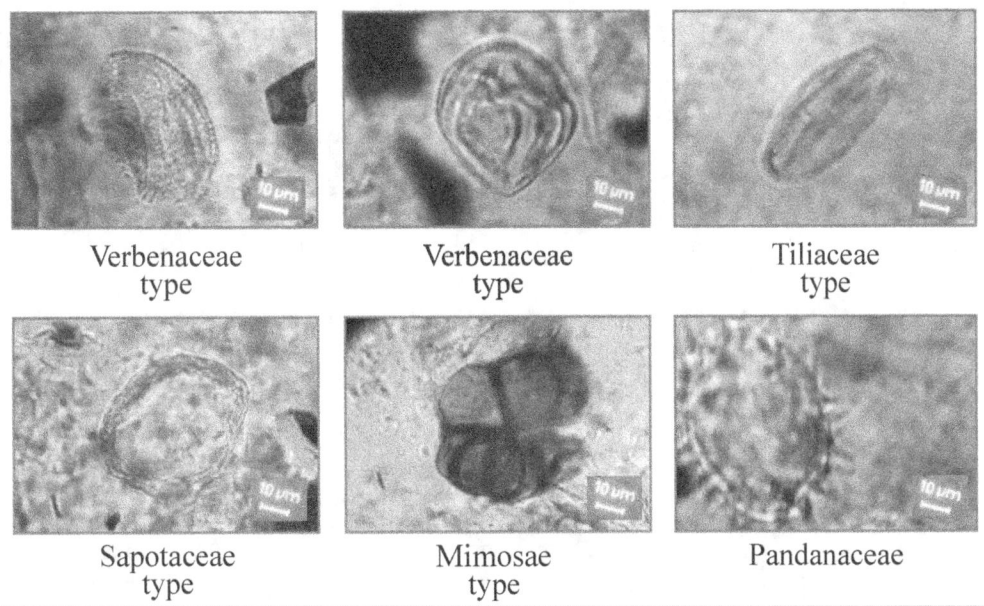

Verbenaceae
type

Verbenaceae
type

Tiliaceae
type

Sapotaceae
type

Mimosae
type

Pandanaceae

Sample 16, 17   **Depth - 80 - 90 cm**

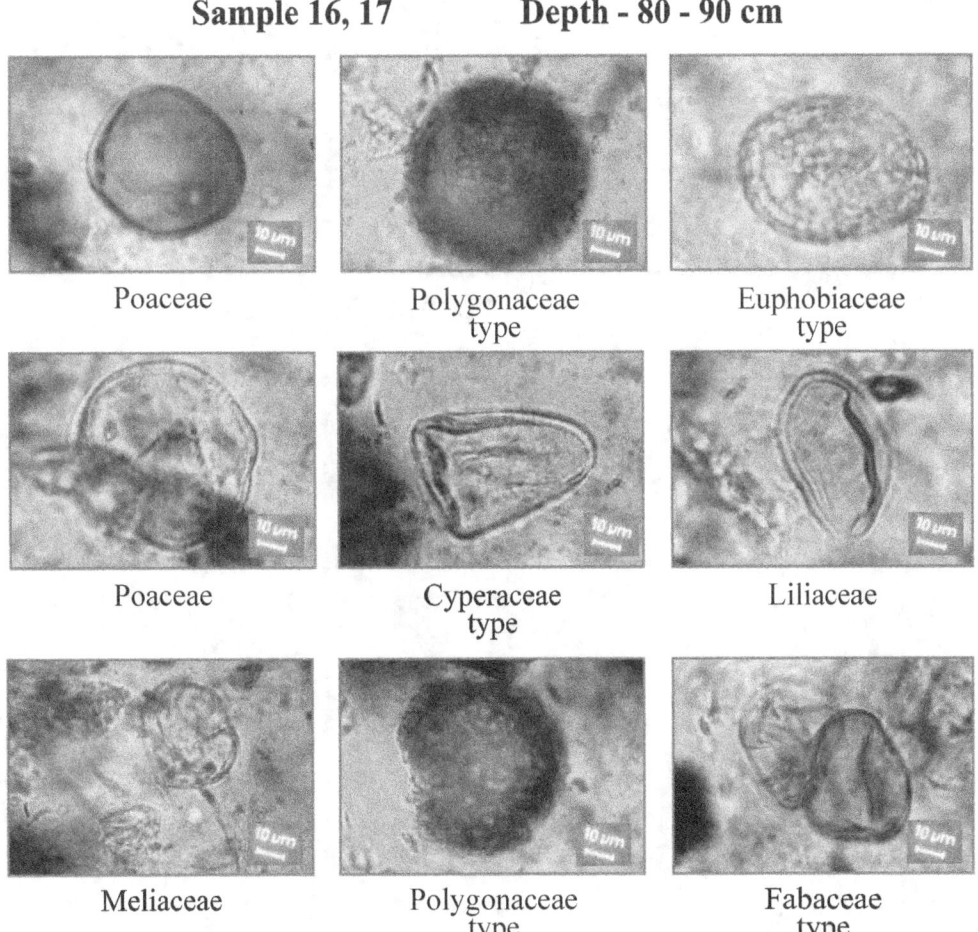

Poaceae

Polygonaceae
type

Euphobiaceae
type

Poaceae

Cyperaceae
type

Liliaceae

Meliaceae

Polygonaceae
type

Fabaceae
type

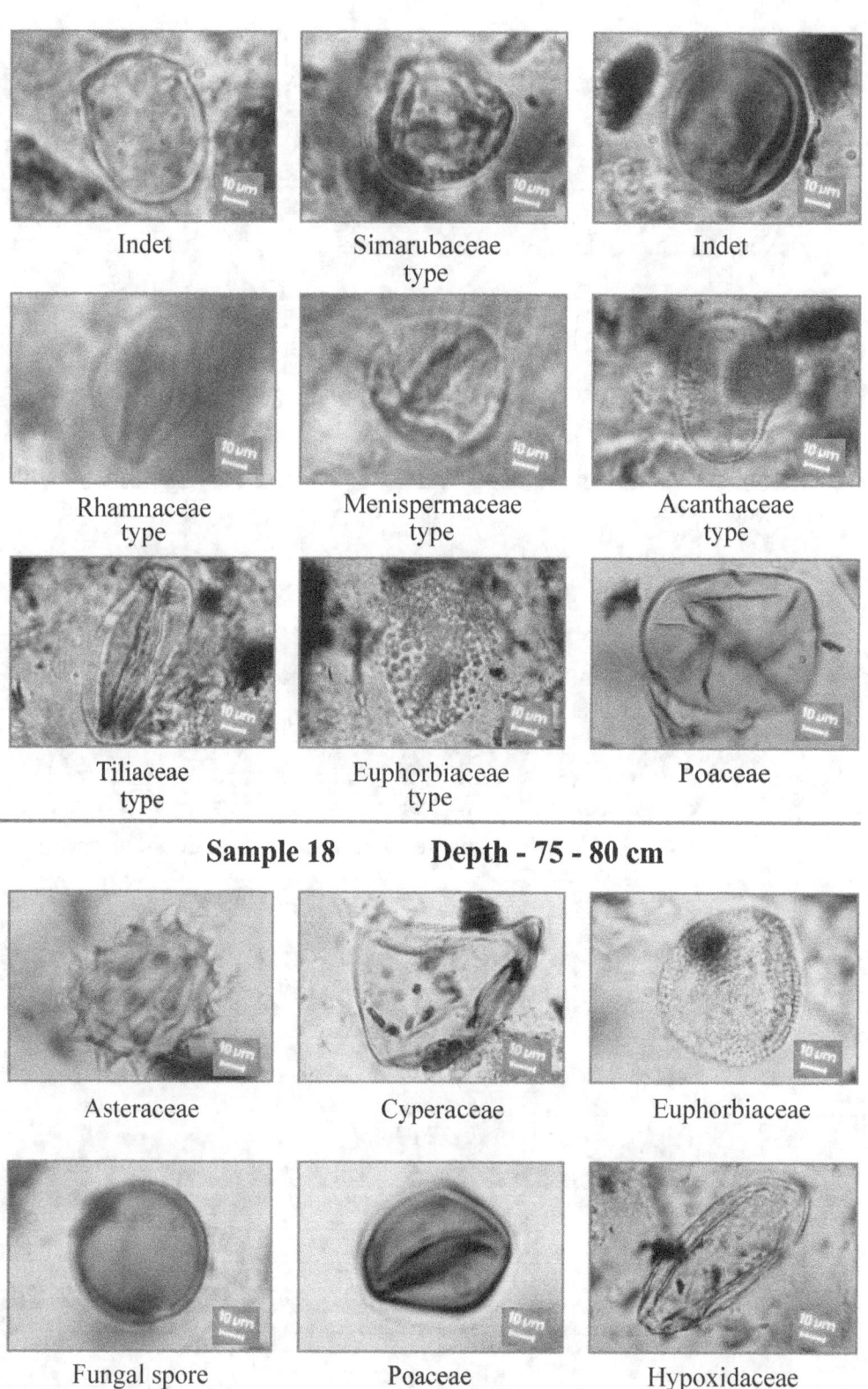

Indet

Simarubaceae type

Indet

Rhamnaceae type

Menispermaceae type

Acanthaceae type

Tiliaceae type

Euphorbiaceae type

Poaceae

Sample 18   Depth - 75 - 80 cm

Asteraceae

Cyperaceae

Euphorbiaceae

Fungal spore

Poaceae

Hypoxidaceae type

FOSSIL POLLEN GRAINS

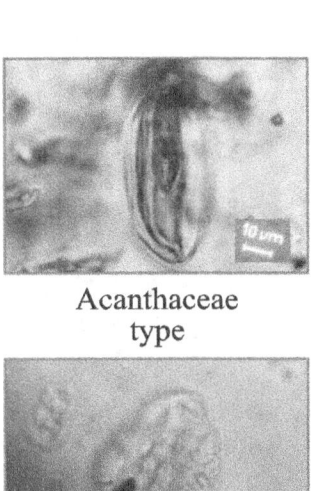
Acanthaceae
type

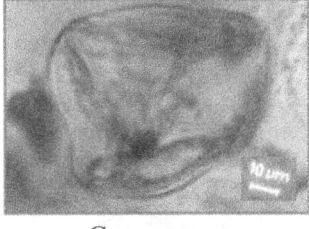
Cyperaceae
type

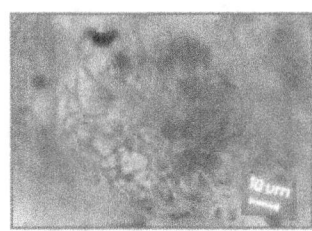
Mimosae
type

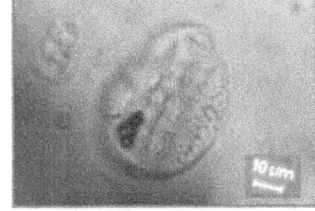
Mimosae

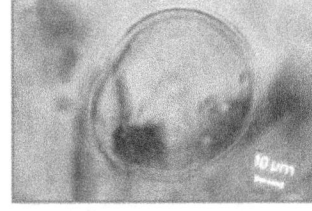
Poaceae

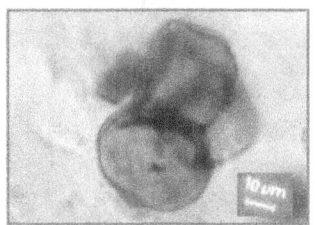
Fungal spores

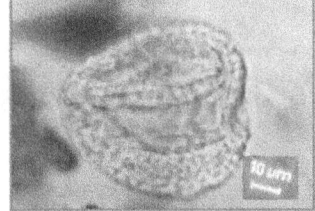
Nymphaeaceae

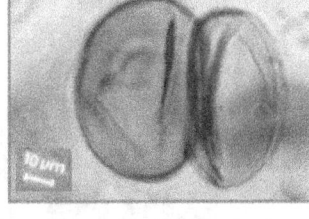
Poaceae / Fabaceae

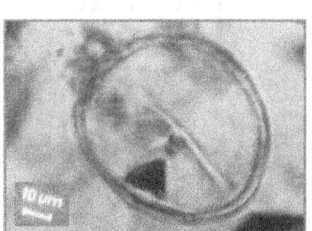
Caesalpiniaceae
type

Sample 19   Depth - 70 - 75 cm

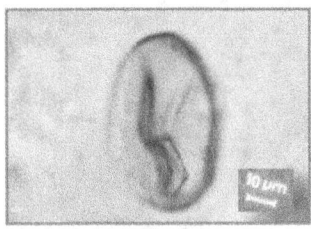
Fabaceae
type

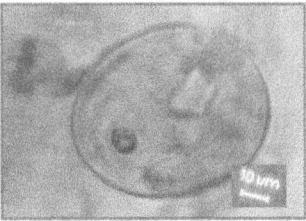
Poaceae

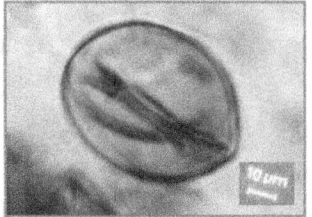
Poaceae
type

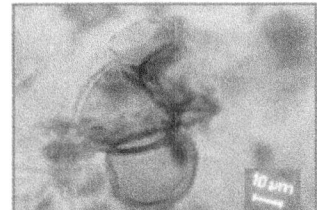
Fungal spores

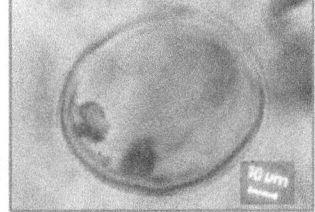
Poaceae

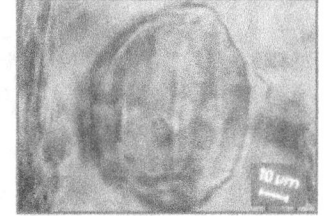
Meliaceae
type

FOSSIL POLLEN GRAINS

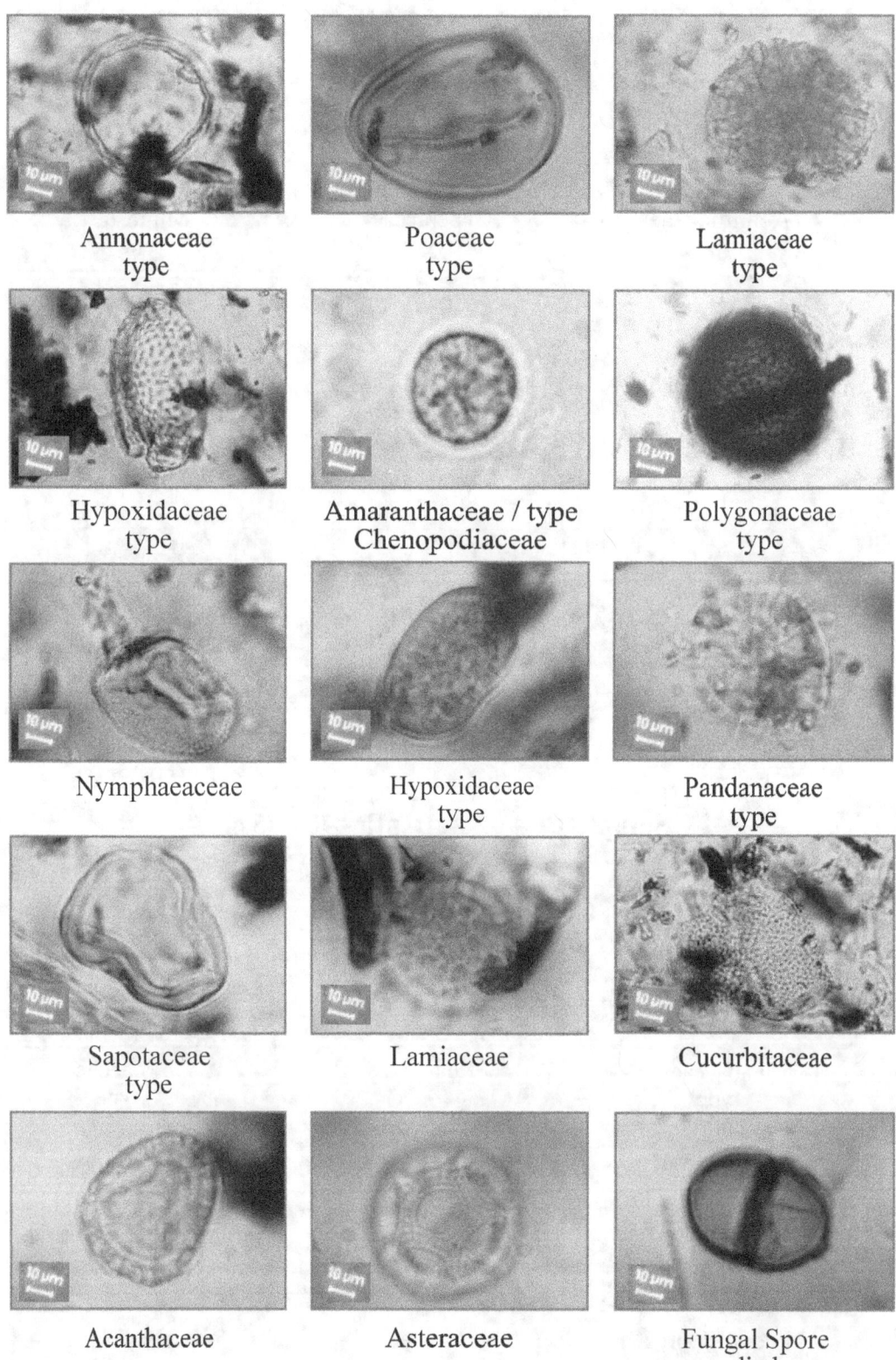

Annonaceae type

Poaceae type

Lamiaceae type

Hypoxidaceae type

Amaranthaceae / type Chenopodiaceae

Polygonaceae type

Nymphaeaceae

Hypoxidaceae type

Pandanaceae type

Sapotaceae type

Lamiaceae

Cucurbitaceae

Acanthaceae

Asteraceae

Fungal Spore diad

ARCHAEOLOGICAL SITE AT MANSAR

**SEMI - LIVE LAKE SITE AT THE
FOOTHILLS OF ARCHAEOLOGICAL SITE**

LAKE SITE AT MANSAR

SHELLS - MNS III
27 cm

Shell assemblage
27 cm - 40 cm

SHELLS - MNS III

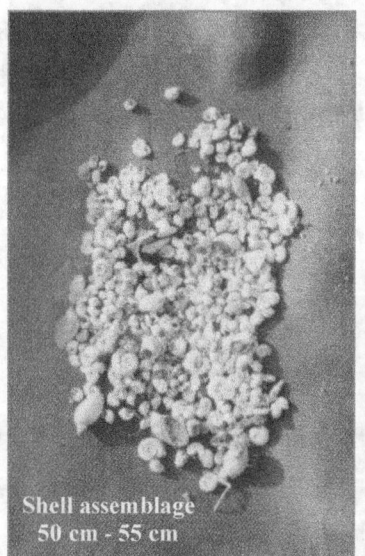

Shell assemblage
50 cm - 55 cm

SHELLS AFTER DRY SIEVING
- MNS III 0-25 cm

Shell assemblage
50 cm - 55 cm

SHELLS - MNS III

RHIZOCONCRETIONS
MNS - II

CALCIUM CARBONATE NODULES.
ENCRUSTED UPON MANGANESE - MNS II (80 cm)

MANGENESE NODULES

APPENDIX

<u>List of plants from Nagpur and Chandrapur region.</u>

Sr.No.	Family	Sr.no. plants.	Botanical Name	Common Name	Habit
1.	Nelumbonaceae	1	*Nelumbo nucifera* Gaertn. syn *Nelumbium speciosum* willd	Kamal	Herb
2.	Nymphaeaceae	2	*Nymphaea nouchali* Burm. syn. *N. stellata* willd.	Nalini	Herb
		3	*Nymphaea pubescens* willd ,syn N . lotus auct .	Himani	Herbs
		4	*Nymphaea nouchali var. cyanea* (Hook. F. and Thoms.)		
3	Annonaceae	5	*Annona squamosa* L.	Sitaphal	Tree
		6	*Polyalthia longifolia* (sonn.) Thw.	Aashok	Tree
		7	*Miliusa tomentosa* (Roxb.)Sinclair. syn *Saccopetalum tomentosum*.		Tree
4	Menispermaceae	8	*Cissampelos pareira* L. var *hirsuta*	Pahadvel	Twiner
		9	*Cocculus hirsutus* (L) Theab. syn *C. villosus*	Jaljamini	Climber
		10	*Tinospora cordifolia* (willd .) Miers ex Hook. f. and Thoms. = *T. glabra*	Gulvel	Climber

Sr.No.	Family	Sr.no. plants.	Botanical Name	Common Name	Habit
5	Capparaceae	11	*Capparis brevispina* DC . syn. *C. zeylanica.*	Govindphal	Shrub
		12	*Capparis decidua* (Forssk.) Edgew. syn. *C. aphylla.*	Nepti	Shrub
		13	*Capparis eleghornii* Dunn ex Gamble, Fl. Syn *C. moonii* var *tomentosa*	Wagati	Climber
		14	*Capparis rotundifolia* Rottl.		Shrub
		15	*Cleome chelidonii* L.f.	Pantilwan	Herb
		16	*Cleome simplicifolia* (camb.) Hook.	Tilvan	Herb
		17	*Cleome viscosa* L.		Herb
		18	*Crateva adansonii* ssp.odora (Buch.-Ham.) Jacobs.	Varun	Tree
		19	*Maerua oblongifolia* (forssk.). A. Rich.		Shrub
6	Papaveraceae	20	*Argemone mexicana* L.	Piwala Dhotra	Herb
7	Cochlospermaceae	21	*Cochlospermum religiosum* (L) Alst. = *C gossypium.*	Ganer	Tree
8	Flacourtiaceae	22	*Casearia rubescens* Dalz.		Shrub
		23	*Flacourtia indica*(Burm. f) Merr .		Shrub
Sr.No.	Family	Sr.no. plants.	Botanical Name	Common Name	Habit
		24	*Flacourtia montana* Grah.		Tree
9	Violaceae	25	*Hybanthus enneaspermus* (L.) F. Muell.		Herb
10	Polygalaceae	26	*Polygala arvensis*. Willd.	Phutani	Herb
		27	*Polygala elongata* Klein.		Herb

Sr.No.	Family	Sr.no. plants	Botanical Name	Common Name	Habit
		28	*Polygala eriopetera* DC.		Herb
11	Portulacaceae	29	*Portulaca oleracea* L.	Gholu	Herb
12	Dipterocarpaceae	30	*Shorea robusta* Roxb.	Saal	Tree
13	Bombacaceae	31	*Bombax ceiba* L.	Katesaveri	Tree
		32	*Bombax insigne* wall.	Savar	Tree
14	Malvaceae	33	*Abutilon indicum* (L.) Sweet , Hort .	Mudra	Shrub
		34	*Decaschistia trilobata* wight , Ic .		Shrub
		35	*Gossypium arboreum* L.	Kapas	Shrub
		36	*Gossypium herbaceum* L.		Shrub
		37	*Hibiscus ceasius* Garcke in Oest .		Herb
		38	*Hibicus rosa – sinensis* L.	Jaswand	Shrub
		39	*Hibiscus hirtus* L.	Dupari	Shrub

Sr.No.	Family	Sr.no. plants.	Botanical Name	Common Name	Habit
		40	*Hibiscus mutabilis* L.	Bhend	Shrub
		41	*Hibiscus panduraeformis* Burm.f .Fl .		Herb
		42	*Hibiscus Obtusilobus Garcke in Oester, Boet . =Hibiscus punctatus Dalz.*		Herb
		43	*Hibiscus ficulneus* (L.)		Shrub
		44	*Hibiscus lobatus (J.A.Murr.) O. Ktze . = Hibiscus solandra*		Herb
		45	*Malachra capitata* (L.) L .		Shrub
		46	*Sida acuta* Burm.f.fl.	Chikna	Shrub
		47	*Sida cordifolia* L.	Kumai	Shrub

145

		48	*Sida ovata* forssk.		Shrub
		49	*Sida cordata (Burm . f .) Borss .* = *Sida veronicifolia* Lamk.		Shrub
		50	*Thespesia lampas* (Cav.) Dalz & Gibs.	Chichundar/ Ranbhendi	Shrub
		51	*Urena lobata* L.	Vanbhendi	Shrub
15	Sterculiac eae	52	*Abroma angusta* (L.)=*Theobroma angusta*	Ulat kambal	Shrub
		53	*Eriolaena candollei* wall	Bothi	Tree

Sr.No.	Family	Sr.no. plants.	**Botanical Name**	Common Name	Habit
		54	*Eriolaena quinquelocularis* (Wright and Arn.)		Tree
		55	*Guazuma ulmifolia* Lam.		Tree
		56	*Helicteres isora* L.	Murudsheng	Shrub
		57	*Melochia corchorifolia* L.		Herb

		58	*Sterculia foetida* L.	Gordada	Tree
		59	*Sterculia guttata* Roxb.		Tree
		60	*Sterculia Urens.* Roxb.Pl. Cor.	Kaudal/ Ghost tree	Tree
		61	*Waltheria indica* L.		Herb
16	Byttneriaceae	62	*Byttneria herbacea* Roxb.		Herb
17	Tiliaceae	63	*Corchorus olitorius* L.		Herb
		64	*Grewia asiatica* L.		Tree
		65	*Grewia abutilifolia* Vent .		Tree
		66	*Grewia damine* Gaertn. syn.*G.salvifolia*	Bihul	Shrub
		67	*Grewia flavescens* A. Juss.	Khatkhati	Shrub

Sr.No.	Family	Sr.no. plants.	Botanical Name	Common Name	Habit
		68	*Grewia serrulata* DC.		Tree
		69	*Grewia tiliifolia* Vahl. .		*Tree*

Sr.No.	Family	Sr.no. plants.	Botanical Name	Common Name	Habit
		70	*Grewia tenax (forssk .) Fiori.*		Shrub
		71	*Triumfetta pilosa* Roth, Nov.		Shrub
		72	*Triumfetta rhomboidea* Jacq.		Herb
		73	*Triumfetta rotundifolia* Lamk.		Shrub
18	Balsaminaceae	74	*Impatiens balsamina.* L.	Terda	Herb
		75	*Impatiens lawii* Hook.f.and Thoms.	Lahan terda	Herb
19	Balanitaceae	76	*Balanites aegyptiaca* (L.) Del. =*B. roxburghii* Planch.	Hinganbet	Tree
20	Rutaceae	77	*Aegle marmelos* (L.) Corr.	Bel	Tree
		78	*Acronychia pedunculata* (L)Miq.		Tree
		79	*Citrus aurantifolia* (Christm. and Panz.) Swingle.	Limbu	Shrub
		80	*Limonia acidissima* L. syn *Feronia elephantum.*	kavath	Tree
21	Flindersiaceae	81	*Chloroxylon swetenia* DC.	Bhirra	Tree
22	Meliaceae	82	*Azadirachta indica* A. Juss.	Neem	Tree
		83	*Melia azedarach* L.	Bakan nimb	Tree
		84	*Soymida febrifuga* (Roxb.) A. Juss.	Rohan	Tree
		85	*Toona hexandra* (Wall. ex Roxb.) Roem.		Tree
Sr.No.	Family	Sr.no. plants.	Botanical Name	Common Name	Habit
23	Burseraceae	86	*Boswellia serrata* Roxb.	Salai	Tree

			Garuga pinnata Roxb.	Kakkad	Tree
		87			
24	Simaroubaceae	88	Ailanthus excelsa Roxb.	Maharukh	Tree
25	Vitaceae	89	Ampelocissus latifolia (Roxb.) planch.		Climber
		90	Ampelocissus ternata (Roth ex R.and S.) DC. syn. Vitis tomentosa.		Shrub
		91	Cissus pallida (Wt and Arn.) Planch.		Shrub
		92	Cissus triloba (Lamk.) Almedia .		Climber
		93	Cissus woodrowii (Stapf ex T. Cooke) Sant.		Shrub
26	Rhamnaceae	94	Scutia myrtina (Burm. f.) Kurz.		Shrub
		95	Ventilago denticulata Willd.	Lokhandi	Climber
		96	Ventilago maderaspatana Gaertn.	Bhingri	Climber
		97	Ziziphus mauritiana Lamk. = Z. jujuba	Bor/Ber	Shrub
		98	Ziziphus oenoplia (L.) Mill.	Yeruni	Shrub
		99	Ziziphus horrida Roth.		Shrub
27	Celastraceae	100	Celastrus paniculatus willd.	Malkanguni	Twiner

Sr.No.	Family	Sr.no. plants.	Botanical Name	Common Name	Habit
		101	*Maytenus rothiana* (walp.) Lobreau – collen. syn. *Gymnosporia rothiana.*	Lokhandi	Shrub
		102	*Maytenus senegalensis* (Lamk.) Excell. syn. *Gymposporia montana.*		Shrub
28	Sapindaceae	103	*Cardiospermum halicacabum* L.	Kapalphodi	Herb
		104	*Dodonea angustifolia* L.f.		Shrub
		105	*Sapindus emarginatus* Vahl. = *S. laurifolius* Vahl.	Ritha	Tree
		106	*Schleichera oleosa* (Lour.) Oken in Allg. = *S. trijuga.*	Kusum	Tree
29	Moringaceae	107	*Moringa oleifera* Lamk. = *M.pterigosperma*	Shevaga	Tree
30	Anacardiaceae	108	*Buchanania cochinchinensis* (Lour.) Almeida, fl.	Charoli	Tree
		109	*Holigarna arnottiana* Hook.f.		Tree
		110	*Lannea coromandelica* (Houtt.) Merr.		Tree
		111	*Mangifera indica* L.	Aamba	Tree
		112	*Semecarpus anacardium* L.f.	Bibba	Tree
31	Droseraceae	113	*Drosera burmanni* Vahl.	Davbindu	Herb
32	Haloragaceae	114	*Myriophyllum oliganthum* (Wt and Arn.)F.v.Muell.		Herb

Sr.No.	Family	Sr.no. plants.	Botanical Name	Common Name	Habit
33	Mimosaceae	115	*Acacia catechu* (L.f.) willd.	Khair	Tree
		116	*Acacia chundra* (Roxb. ex Rottl.) willd.		Tree

		117	*Acacia ferruginea* DC.	Pandhra khair	Tree
		118	*Acacia nilotica* (L.) willd .	Babhul	Tree
		119	*Albizia lebbeck* (L.) Bth.	Siras	Tree
		120	*Albizia odoratissima* (L.f.) Bth.	Kala siras	Tree
		121	*Albizia procera* (Roxb) Bth.	Safed siras	Tree
		122	*Dichrostachys cinerea* (L.) wt.and Arn . var *indica*.	Sigam kati/Durangi	Shrub
		123	*Mimosa hamata* Willd.	Arati	Shrub
		124	*Mimosa pudica* L.	Lajari	Herb
		125	*Pithecollobium dulce* (Roxb) Bth.	Vilayti chinch	Tree
		126	*Prosopis cineraria* (L.) Druce.	Shemi/Wedi Babhul	Tree
		127	*Xylia xylocarpa* (Roxb.Taub.)		Tree
34	Fabaceae	128	*Aeschynomene indica* L.		Herb

Sr.No.	Family	Sr.no. plants.	Botanical Name	Common Name	Habit

		129	*Abrus precatorius* L.	Pandhara Gunj	Twiner
		130	*Aeschynomene americana* L.		Shrub
		131	*Aeschynomene aspera* L.		Shrub
		132	*Alysicarpus ovalifolius* (schum.) J. Leon.		Herb
		133	*Alysicarpus vaginalis* (L.) DC. var *nummularifolius.*		Herb
		134	*Butea monosperma* (Lamk.) Taub.*var.lutea* (Witt) Mahesh.	Palas	Tree
		135	*Butea superba* Roxb.	Palas -vel	Climber
		136	*Crotalaria mysorensis* Roth.		Herb
		137	*Crotalaria pusilla* Heyne ex DC.		Herb
		138	*Crotalaria retusa* L.	Dingla	Herb
		139	*Cajanus cajan* (L.) Millsp.	Tur	Shrub
		140	*Cajanus scarabaeoides* (L.) du-petit Thours.	Rantur	Herb
		141	*Canavalia ensiformis* (L.) DC.		Climber

Sr.No.	Family	Sr.no. plants.	Botanical Name	Common Name	Habit
		142	*Clitorea ternatea* L. var *ternatea.*	Gokarn	Twiner
		143	*Crotalaria hebecarpa* (DC.) Rudd. syn. *Heylandia latebrosa.*	Godhadi	Herb
		144	*Crotalaria linifolia* L.f.		Herb
		145	*Cullen corylifolia* (L.) Medik. Syn. *Psoralea corylifolia* L.	Bavchi	Herb
		146	*Dalbergia latifolia* Roxb.	Shisav	Tree
		147	*Dalbergia sissoo* Roxb.	Shisham	Tree
		148	*Derris scandens* (Roxb.) Bth.		Climber
		149	*Desmodium gangeticum* (L.) DC.		Shrub
		150	*Desmodium velutinum* (Willd.)DC. syn *D. latifolium.*		Shrub
		151	*Desmodium laxiflorum* DC.		Shrub
		152	*Desmodium alysicarpoides* Van Meeuwen. syn *D. parviflorum*		Shrub
		153	*Desmodium triflorum* (L.) DC.		Herb
		154	*Dumasia villosa* DC.		Herb
		155	*Erythrina variegata* L. var *variegata*	Pangara	Tree
Sr.No.	Family	Sr.no. plants.	Botanical Name	Common Name	Habit
		156	*Flemingia strobilifera* (L.)Ait.and Ait. syn *F. Bracteata.*		Shrub
		157	*Flemingia involucrata* Bth in miq Pl Jungh		Herb
		158	*Flemingia semialata* Roxb.		Shrub
		159	*Geissaspis cristata* Wt and Arn. var *tenella* (Bth.) Almedia.	Lahan barki	Herb
		160	*Indigofera liniafolia* (L.) Retz.		Herb
		161	*Indigofera astragalina* DC.Syn.*I hirsuta.*		Shrub

		162	*Indigofera cordifolia* Heyne ex Roth.		Herb
		163	*Indigofera dalzellii* T. Cooke.		Herb
		164	*Indigoferacassioides* Rottl. Ex DC. syn. *pulchella* .		Shrub
		165	*Melilotus alba* Medik.ex.Desr.		Herb
		166	*Mucuna pruriens* (L.) DC.	Kaunch	Twiner
		167	*Pueraria montana* (Lour.) Merr.		Twiner
		168	*Pongamia pinnata* (L.) Pierre .	Karanj	Tree
		169	*Pseudarthria viscida* (L.) Wight and Arn. =*S. grandifolia*		Shrub

Sr.No.	Family	Sr.no. plants.	Botanical Name	Common Name	Habit
		170	*Sesbania bispinosa* (Jacq.) W.F. Wt.		Shrub
		171	*Shuteria vestita* (Grah.in Wall.)) Wight and Arn.		Twiner
		172	*Tephrosia pupurea* (L.) Pers.		Shrub
		173	*Teramnus labialis* (L.f.) spreng.		Twiner
		174	*Tephrosia tinctoria* (L.) Pers.		Shrub
35	Caesalpiniaceae	175	*Bauhinia semla* Wanderlin.		Tree
		176	*Bauhinia vahlii* wight and Arn.		Climber
		177	*Bauhinia variegata* L.	Pandhra kanchan	Tree
		178	*Cassia tora* L.	Tarota	Herb
		179	*Cassia minosoides* L.		Herb
		180	*Cassia surattensis* Burm f.		Shrub
		181	*Caesalpinia bonduc* (L.) Roxb.	Gajara	Shrub
		182	*Cassia occidentalis* L.	Kasivda	Shrub
		183	*Cassia fistula* L.	Bahava	Tree
		184	*Cassia sophera* L.	Deotarotha	Shrub
		185	*Hardwickia binata* Roxb.	Anjan	Tree
		186	*Parkinsonia aculeata* L.	Wedi babhul	Shrub

Sr.No.	Family	Sr.no. plants.	Botanical Name	Common Name	Habit
		187	*Tamarindus indica* L.	Chinch	Tree
36	Combretaceae	188	*Anogeissus latifolia* (Roxb.ex DC.) Wall.	Dhawda	Tree
		189	*Calycopteris floribunda* (Roxb.) Poir.	Ukashi	Twiner
		190	*Combretum albidum* G. Don. =*C. ovalifolium*	Madbel	Twiner
		191	*Terminalia catappa* L.	Deshibadam	Tree
		192	*Terminalia chebula* Retz.	Hirda	Tree
		193	*Terminalia cuneata* Roth	Arjun sadda	Tree
		194	*Terminalia elliptica* willd. =*T.Tomentosa.*		Tree
		195	*Terminalia bellirica* (Gaertn) Roxb.	Behda	Tree
37	Melastomataceae	196	*Osbeckia muralis* naud . = *O. truncata*		Herb
38	Onagraceae	197	*Ludwigia hyssopifolia* (G. Don) Exell.		Herb
		198	*Ludwigia octovalvis* (Jacq.) Raven.		Herb
39	Lythraceae	199	*Ammannia octandra* L.f.		Herb
		200	*Lagerstroemia microcarpa* Wight.		Tree
		201	*Lagerstroemia parviflora* Roxb.		Tree
		202	*Lagerstromia speciosa* Roxb. = *L.reginae*	Motha bandhara	Tree

Sr.No.	Family	Sr.no. plants.	Botanical Name	Common Name	Habit
		203	*Rotala fimbriata* Wight.		Herb
		204	*Rotala indica* (willd.) Koehne.		Herb
		205	*Woodfordia fruticosa* (L.) Kurz.	Dhaiti	Shrub
40	Myrtaceae	206	*Syzygium cumini* (L.) Skeels.	Jambhul	Tree
		207	*Syzygium rubicundum* Wight and Arn.		Tree
41	Lecythidaceae	208	*Careya arborea* Roxb.	Kumbohya	Tree

Sr.No.	Family	Sr.no. plants.	Botanical Name	Common Name	Habit
42	Cucurbitaceae	209	*Diplocyclos palmatus* (L.) C.Jeffrey syn *Bryonopsis laciniosa*	Shankar pindi	Climber
		210	*Coccinia grandis* (L.) Voigt. syn *C.indica*	Tondali	Climber
		211	*Momordica dioica* Roxb ex Willd.	Kartoli	Climber
		212	*Mukia maderaspatana* (L.) Roem. =*Melothria maderaspatana*	Chirati	Climber
		213	*Trichosanthes cucumerina* L.	Jungli padval	Climber
		214	*Trichosanthes tricuspidata* Lour	Kaundal	Climber
43	Trapaceae	215	*Trapa natans* L. var *bispinosa*	Shingada	Herb
44	Cactaceae	216	*Nopalea cochenillifera* (L.) Salm.Dyck.	Nagphani	Shrub
45	Molluginaceae	217	*Mollugo pentaphylla* L.		Herb
Sr.No.	Family	Sr.no. plants.	**Botanical Name**	Common Name	Habit
46	Apiaceae	218	*Seseli diffusum* (Roxb.ex.J.E.Sm) Sant.and Wagh.		Herb
47	Alangiaceae	219	*Alangium salvifolium* (L.f.) Wang.		Tree
48	Rubiaceae	220	*Catunaregum spinosa* (Thunb.) Tirveng. =*Gardenia spinosa*	Gela	Shrub
		221	*Ceriscodies turgida* (Roxb.) Tirveng. =*Gardenia turgida*	Phetra	Tree
	Rubiaceae	222	*Dentella repens* (L.) J. R. & G.forst. syn *Oldenlandia repens* .		Herb
		223	*Gardenia gummifera* L.f = *G. lucida*	Dikemali	Tree
		224	*Gardenia latifolia* Soland.	Kala hetera	Tree
		225	*Gardenia resinifera* Roth.		Tree
		226	*Haldina cordifolia* (Roxb) Ridsd. syn *Adina cordifolia*		Shrub
		227	*Hedyotis corymbosa* (L) Lamk. syn *Oldenlandia corymbosa*		Herb

		228	*Hedyotis stocksii* (Hook.f.homs) Rao and Hemadri.		Herb
		229	*Ixora brachiata* Roxb.		Tree

Sr.No.	Family	Sr.no. plants.	Botanical Name	Common Name	Habit
		230	*Ixora coccinea* L.	Bakara	Shrub
		231	*Ixora pavetta* Andr. = *I. arborea*	Hemadri	Shrub
		232	*Mitragyna parvifolia* (Roxb.) Korth.		Tree
		233	*Morinda pubescens* J.E.Sm.		Tree
		234	*Rubia cordifolia* L.		Twiner
		235	*Spermacoce ocymoides* Burm.f.		Herb
		236	*Spermacoce pusilla* Wall. = *S.stricta*		Herb
49	Asteraceae	237	*Ageratum conyzoides* L.	Osadi	Herb
		238	*Anaphalis lawii* (Hook.f.) Gamble.		Herb
		239	*Bidens sulphurea* (Cav.) Sch-Bip. syn. *Cosmos sulphureus* .		Herb
		240	*Blumea obliqua* .(L.) Druce .		Herb
		241	*Blumea lacera* (Burm.f.) DC.		Herb
		242	*Blumea mollis* (D.Don) Merr.		Herb
		243	*Caesulia axillaris* Roxb.	Mala	Herb
		244	*Conyza stricta* willd.	Batdavana	Herb
		245	*Sonchus brachyotus* DC.		Herb

Sr.No.	Family	Sr.no. plants.	Botanical Name	Common Name	Habit
		246	*Eclipta prostrata* (L.) L. syn *E. alba.*	Burngaraj	Herb
		247	*Echinops echinatus* Roxb.		Herb
		248	*Elephantopus scaber* L.	Hastipat	Herb
		249	*Emilia sonchifolia* (L.) DC.		Herb
		250	*Epaltes divaricata* (L.) Cass.		Herb
		251	*Grangea maderaspatana* (L.) Poir.	Mashipatri	Herb
		252	*Gnaphalium luteo-album* L.		Herb
		253	*Lactuca remotiflora* DC.	Patheri	Herb
	Asteraceae	254	*Lagascea mollis* Cav.	Tharvad	Herb
		255	*Parthenium hysterophorus* L.	Gajargavat	Herb
		256	*Pentanema cernuum* (Dalz.) Ling	Sonsari	Herb
		257	*Pentanema indicum* (L.) Ling.	Sonkadi	Herb
		258	*Sphaeranthus indicus* L.		Herb
		259	*Tricholepis radican* (Roxb.DC.	Dhhan	Herb
		260	*Tridax procumbens* L.	Dagadi pala	Herb
		261	*Xanthium indicum* koen.	Shankeshvar	Herb
50	Lobeliaceae	262	*Lobelia alsinoides* Lam.		Herb
51	Campanulaceae	263	*Wahlenbergia marginata* (Thunb.) A.DC.		Herb
52	Plumbaginaceae	264	*Plumbago zeylanica* L.	Chitrak	Shrub
Sr.No.	Family	Sr.no. plants.	Botanical Name	Common Name	Habit
53	Ebenaceae	265	*Diospyros melanoxylon.* Roxb.	Temru	Tree
54	Sapotaceae	266	*Mimusops elengi* L.	Bakul	Tree
		267	*Madhuca indica* Gmel. =*Bassia latifolia*	Mahua	Tree
		268	*Madhuca longifolia* (Koen.) Mac Bride. = *B.longifolia.*		Tree
		269	*Manikara hexandra* (Roxb.) Dub.	Khirni	Tree

Sr.No.	Family	Sr.no. plants.	Botanical Name	Common Name	Habit
55	Menyanthaceae	270	*Nymphoides indicum* (L) O.Ktze.		Herb
		271	*Nymphoides hydrophylla* (Lout) O.Ktze		Herb
56	Solanaceae	272	*Physalis angulata* L.=*P. minima*	Ranpopti	Herb
		273	*Physalis longifolia* Nutt.		Herb
		274	*Solanum virginianum* L.	Kate -ringni	Herb
57	Convolvulaceae	275	*Argyreia sericea* Dalz. And Gibs.	Gavel	Twiner
		276	*Convolvulus arvensis* L.	Chandvel	Herb
		278	*Evolvulus nummularis* (L.) L.		Herb
		279	*Ipomoea aquatica* Forssk.	Nilichi bhaji	Shrub
		280	*Ipomoea pes-tigrides* L.	Panchapatri	Twiner

Sr.No.	Family	Sr.no. plants.	Botanical Name	Common Name	Habit
		281	*Ipomoea nil* (L.) Roth.	Nil	Twiner
		282	*Ipomoea clarkei* Hook.f.		Twiner
		283	*Ipomoea eriocarpa* R. Br.		Twiner
		284	*Ipomoea hederifolia* L.		Twiner
		285	*Ipomoea obscura* (L.) Ker-Gawl.		Twiner
		286	*Merremia hederacea* Burm.f.Hall.f. =*Merremia chryseides.*	Himali	Twiner
		287	*Operculina tansaensis* Sant and Patel.		Twiner
		288	*Operculina turpethum* (L.) S.		Twiner
		289	*Rivea hypocrateriformis* (Desr.) Choisy.	Phangyel	Climber
		290	*Xenostegia tridentata* (L.) Austin and staples.		Herb
58	Boraginaceae	291	*Coldenia procumbens* L.	Tripanki	Herb
		292	*Cordia dichotoma* Forst.f.	Bhokar	Tree
		293	*Cordia macleodii.* (Griff.) Hook. f.	Dahivan	Tree
		294	*Ehertia aspera* Roxb.		Tree
		295	*Heliotropium indicum* L.		Herb
		296	*Trichodesma zeylanicum* (Burm.f.) R.Br.	Jalshirasi	Herb

Sr.No.	Family	Sr.no. plants.	Botanical Name	Common Name	Habit
		297	*Trichodesma indicum* (L.) Lehm.	Pataldhundi	Herb
59	Oleaceae	298	*Chionanthus mala-elengi* (Dennst.) P.S.Green.	Heddi	Tree
		299	*Nyctanthes arbor-tristis* L.	Parijatak	Tree
		300	*Olax psittacorum* (Willd.) Vahl		Shrub
		301	*Schrebera swieteniodes* Roxb.	Mokha/ Goki	Tree
60	Gentianaceae	302	*Canscora decussata* (Roxb.) J.A.and H.Schult.		Herb
		303	*Canscora diffusa* (Vahl) R.Br.ex.R.and S.		Herb
		304	*Enicostema axillare* (Lam.) Raynal.	Mamejav	Herb
		305	*Exacum petiolare* Griseb.	Nili chirayat	Herb
61	Asclepiadaceae	306	*Asclepias curassavica* L.		Herb
		307	*Calotropis gigantea* (L.) Ait.	Rui	Shrub
		308	*Oxylstelma esculentum* (L.f.) R.Br.	Dudhani	Twiner
		309	*Pergularia daemia* (Forssk.) Choiv.	Utrani	Shrub
		310	*Telosma pallida* (Roxb.) Craib.		Twiner
62	Periplocaceae	311	*Cryptolepis buchanani* Roem and Schult .	Kavali	Climber
63	Apocynaceae	312	*Alstonia scholaris* (L.) R.Br.	Satvin	Tree
		313	*Catharanthus pussilus* (Murr.) G.Don.	Sangkhi	Herb
		314	*Holarrhena pubesens* (Buch-Ham) Wall.ex G.Don. Syn *H. antidysentrica*.	Pandhara kuda	Shrub

Sr.No.	Family	Sr.no. plants.	Botanical Name	Common Name	Habit
		315	*Quirivelia frutescens* (L.) M.R.and S.M.Almeida. Syn *Ichnocarpus frutescens* .		Twiner
		316	*Tabernaemontana alternifolia* (Roxb.) Nicols.and Suresh.	Nagkuda	Shrub
		317	*Wrightia tinctoria* R.Br.	Kala kuda	Tree

160

Sr.No.	Family	Sr.no. plants.	Botanical Name	Common Name	Habit
64	Lentibulariaceae	318	*Utricularia exoleta* R.Br.		Herb
		319	*Utricularia bifida* L.		Herb
		320	*Utricularia stellaris* L.f.		Herb
65	Bignoniaceae	321	*Dolichandrone falcata* (Wall.ex DC.) Seem.	Medsingi	Tree
		322	*Oroxylum indicum* (L.) Vent.	Tetu	Tree
		323	*Radermachera xylocarpa* (Roxb.K.Schum.	Khadsingh	Tree
		324	*Stereospermum colais* (Buch. -Ham.ex Dillw.) Mabb.	Padal	Tree
66	Scrophulariaceae	325	*Bacopa monnieri* (L.) Penn.	Bramhi	Herb
		326	*Buchnera hispida* Buch. -Ham.ex D.Don.		Herb
		327	*Limnophila indica* (L.) Druce.	Tarti	Herb
		328	*Mazus pumilus* (Burm.f.) Steenis. syn *Mazus rugosus* .		Herb
		329	*Sopubia delphinifolia* (L.) G.Don.	Dudhani	Herb
		330	*Stemodia viscosa* Roxb.	Satmodi	Herb
Sr.No.	Family	Sr.no. plants.	Botanical Name	Common Name	Habit
		331	*Striga asiatica* (L.) O Ktze.		Herb
		332	*Striga gesnerioides* (Willd.) Valke.	Bambakhu	Herb
		333	*Verbascum chinense* (L.) Sant. syn *Celsia coromandeliana*	Kutaki	Herb
67	Thunbergiaceae	334	*Thunbergia laevis* Nees.		Twiner
68	Acanthaceae	335	*Andrographis paniculata* (Burm.f.) Wall.ex Nees.	Kadechiraiet	Herb
		336	*Asystasia dalzelliana* Sant.syn *A. violacea.*		Herb
		337	*Barleria cristata* L.		herb
		338	*Barleria prattensis* Sant.	Gulabi koranti	Shrub
		339	*Barleria prionitis* L.	Kate koranti	Shrub
		340	*Blepharis maderaspatensis* (L.) Roth.		Herb
		341	*Blepharis repens* (Vahl) Roth. Syn *B.molluginifolia*		Herb

Sr.No.	Family	Sr.no. plants.	Botanical Name	Common Name	Habit
		342	*Cynarospermum asperrimum* (Nees) Vollesen. syn *Blepharis asperima*		Herb
		343	*Dicliptera foetida* (Forssk.) Blatt.		Herb
		344	*Ecbolium ligustrinum* (Vahl) Vollesen.		Herb

Sr.No.	Family	Sr.no. plants.	Botanical Name	Common Name	Habit
		345	*Eranthemum roseum* (Vahl.) R.Br.	Ranaboli	Shrub
		346	*Haplanthodes verticillata* (Roxb). R.B. Mujumdar		Herb
		347	*Hemigraphis hirta* (Vahl) T.And.		Herb
		348	*Hygrophila schulii* (Buch-Ham.) M.R.and S.M.Almeida.	Talimkhana	Herb
		349	*Hygrophila ringens* (L.) Steud.		Herb
		350	*Indoneesiella echioides* (L.) Sreem.	Pandhara feda	Shrub
		351	*Justicia adhatoda* L.	Adulsa	Shrub
		352	*Justicia glauca* Rottl.		Herb
		353	*Lepidagathis cristata* Willd	Bhuigend	Herb
		354	*Lepidagathis cuspidata* Nees.		Shrub
		355	*Nelsonia canescens* (Lam.) Spreng.		Herb
		356	*Peristrophe paniculata* (Forssk.) Brummitt Syn *P. bicaculata* Forssk.		Shrub
		357	*Rostellularia diffusa* (Willd.)Nees. Var *prostrata*		Herb
		358	*Rungia pectinata* (L) Nees in DC.		Herb
		359	*Rungia repens* (L.) Nees in Wall.	Pittapapda	Herb
		360	*Staurogyne glauca* (Nees.) O.Ktze.		Herb

Sr.No.	Family	Sr.no. plants.	Botanical Name	Common Name	Habit
69	Martyniaceae	361	*Dipteracanthus patalus* (Jacq.) Nees = *Ruellia patula* Jacq.		Herb

Sr.No.	Family	Sr.no. plants.	Botanical Name	Common Name	Habit
		362	*Martynia annua* L.	Waghnakhi	Herb
70	Lamiaceae	363	*Anisomeles indica* (L.) O.Ktze.		Herb
		364	*Hyptis suaveolens* (L.) Poit.		Herb
		365	*Leonotis nepetiifolia* (L.) R.Br.	Dipmal	Shrub
		366	*Leucas aspera* (Willd.) Link.	Burumbi	Herb
		367	*Leucas zeylanica* (L.) R.Br.		Herb
		368	*Nepeta hindostana* (Heyne ex Roth) Haines.		Herb
		369	*Ocimum americanum* L.		Shrub
		370	*Ocimum basilicum* L.	Rantulas	Herb
		371	*Ocimum tenuiflorum* L.		Shrub
		372	*Ocimum gratissimum* L.		Shrub
		373	*Orthosiphon pallidus* Royle ex Benth.		Herb
		374	*Scutellaria discolor* Wall.ex Bth.		Herb
71	Verbenaceae	375	*Callicarpa tomentosa* (L.) Murr.		Tree
		376	*Clerodendrum inerme* (L.) Gaertn.		Shrub
		377	*Clerodendrum multiflorum* (Burm.f) O.Ktze.	Takalani	Shrub
		378	*Clerodendrum.serratum* (L.) Moon.	Bharangi	Shrub
Sr.No.	Family	Sr.no. plants.	Botanical Name	Common Name	Habit
		379	*Clerodendrum viscosum* Vent.	Bhandiara	Shrub
		380	Gmelina arborea Roxb	Shivan	Tree
		381	*Lantana camara* L.	Ghaneri	Shrub
		382	*Phyla nodiflora* (L.) Greene		Herb
		383	*Premna obtusifolia* R.Br.		Twiner
		384	*Stachytarpheta jamaicensis* (L.) Vahl.		Shrub
		385	*Tectona grandis* L.	Sagwan	Tree
		386	*Vitex negundo* (L.) Domin.	Nirgudi	Shrub
		387	*Vitex trifolia* L.		Shrub
72	Symphoremataceae	388	*Symphorema involucratum* Roxb.		Twiner

163

Sr.No.	Family	Sr.no. plants.	Botanical Name	Common Name	Habit
73	Loranthaceae	389	*Dendrophthoe falcata* (L.f) Etting	Dandgul	Shrub
74	Nyctaginaceae	390	*Boerhavia repens* L. var *diffusa* (L.) Hook.	Khaparphuti	Shrub
75	Polygonaceae	391	*Antigonon leptopus* Hook & Arn.	Icecream creeper	Climber
		392	*Persicaria glabra* (Willd.) Gomez syn *Polygonum glabrum* Willd.	Paral	Herb
		393	*Polygonum plebium* R.Br.		Herb
76	Amaranthaceae	395	*Amaranthus hypochondriacus* L.		Herb

Sr.No.	Family	Sr.no. plants.	Botanical Name	Common Name	Habit
		396	*Amaranthus spinosus* L.	Katemath	Herb
		397	*Achyranthes aspera* L.	Aaghada	Herb
		398	*Allmania nodiflora* (L.) R.Br.		Herb
		399	*Alternanthera sessilis* (L) R.Br.		Herb
		400	*Digera muricata* (L.) Mart.		Herb
		401	*Gomphrena serrata* L.	Patur	Herb
		402	*Pupalia lappacea* (L) A.L.Juss.		Herb
		403	*Trichuriella monsoniae* (L.f) Bennet.		Herb
77	Chenopodiaceae	404	*Atriplex hortensis* L.	Chandan batwa	Herb
		405	*Chenopodium album* L.	Dhanbhaji	Herb
78	Euphorbiaceae	406	*Acalypha ciliata* Forssk.		Herb
		407	*Actephila excelsa* (Dalz.) Muell-Arg.	Garadi	Shrub
		408	*Antidesma acidum* Retz.		Shrub
		409	*Antidesma ghaesembilla* Gaertn.		Shrub
		410	*Baliospermum montanum* (willd.) Muell-Arg.		Shrub
		411	*Bridelia retusa* (L.) Spreng.	Aasana	Shrub

		412	*Bridelia squamosa* (Lam.) Gehrm.		
					Shrub

Sr.No.	Family	Sr.no. plants.	Botanical Name	Common Name	Habit
		413	*Chrozophora rottleri* (Gies) Juss.		Herb
		414	*Cleistanthus collinus* (Roxb.) Both.ex Hook.		Shrub
	Euphorbiaceae	415	*Cleistanthus malabaricus* Muell- Arg.		Shrub
		416	*Euphorbia antiquorum* L.	Tidhari	Herb
		417	*Euphorbia geniculata* Orteg.	Dudhani	Herb
		418	*Euphorbia hirta* L.	Dudhnali	Herb
		419	*Emblica officinalis* Gaertn. =syn Phyllanthus imblica	Avala	Tree
		420	.		
		421	*Jatropa nana* Dalz.		Shrub
		422	*Jatropha curcas* L.		Herb
		423	*Kirganelia reticulata* (Poiret) Baiilon.	Pitauri	Shrub
		424	*Phyllanthus scabrifolius* Hook.f		Herb
		425	*Securinega leucopyrus* (Willd.) Muell. -Arg.		Shrub
		426	*Securinega virosa* (Roxb. ex Willd.) Baill.	Pandhar phalli	Shrub
79	Santalaceae	427	*Santalum album* L.	Chandan	Tree

Sr.No.	Family	Sr.no. plants.	Botanical Name	Common Name	Habit
		428	*Osyris quadripartita* Salz.		Shrub
80	Moraceae	429	*Artocarpus heterophyllus* Lam.	Phanas	Tree
		430	*Ficus benghalensis* L.	Wad	Tree
		431	*Ficus hispida* L.	Bhui umbar	Tree
		432	*Ficus racemosa* L.	Umber	Tree
		433	*Ficus religiosa* L.	Pimpal	Tree
		434	*Ficus virens* Ait.	Payer	Tree
		435	*Morus alba* L.	Tuti	Tree
		436	*Streblus asper* Lour.		Tree
81	Orchidaceae	437	*Habenaria commelinifolia* (Roxb.) Wall.	Aamri	Herb
		438	*Habenaria marginata* Coleb.		Herb
		439	*Habenaria plantaginea* Lindl.		Herb
		440	*Habenaria roxburghii* Nicols		Herb
		441	*Vanda tessellata* (Roxb) Hook.	Rasna	Herb
82	Hydrocharitaceae	442	*Hydrilla verticillata* (L.f.) Royle,III		Herb
		443	*Lagarosiphon alternifolia* (Roxb.) Druce in Rep. syn *Nechaunandra alternifolia*		Herb
		444	*Ottelia alismoides* (L.) Pers.		Herb
		445	*Vallisneria spiralis* L.		Herb
Sr.No.	Family	Sr.no. plants.	Botanical Name	Common Name	Habit
83	Commelinaceae	446	*Commelina attenuata* Koen.		Herb
		447	*Commeliana benghalensis* L.	Kenhe	Herb
		448	*Commeliana forsskalaei* Vahl, Enum.		Herb
		449	*Commelina maculata* Edgew.	Kenhe	Herb
		450	*Murdannia dimorpha* (Dalz.) Brueck. = *Aneilema paniculata* Cl.		Herb
		451	*Murdania nudiflora* (L.) Brenan.		Herb

		452	*Murdannia versicolor* (Dalz.) Brueck. .		Herb
		453	*Tonningia axillaris* (L.) O. Ktze.		Herb
84	Smilacaceae	454	*Eichhornia crassipes* (Mart.) Solms.	Jalaparni	Herb
		455	*Smilax ovalifolia* Roxb.	Bachnag	Climber
85	Liliaceae	456	*Aloe vera* (L.) Burm.	Korphad	Shrub
		457	*Asparagus racemosus* Willd.	Shatavari	Herb
		458	*Chlorophytum borivilianum* Sant & fernand.		Herb
		459	*Chlorophytum tubersum* (Roxb.) Baker.		Herb
		460	*Cordyline terminalis* Kunth.Enum.		Shrub
		461	*Gloriosa superba* L.	Agnishikha	Climber
		462	*Iphigenia pallida* Baker in J.	Bhuitara	Herb

Sr.No.	Family	Sr.no. plants.	Botanical Name	Common Name	Habit
		463	*Protasperagus racemosus* (Willd.)Oberm.	Shatavari	Herb
		464	*Scilla hyacinthina* (Roth) Mc Bride.	Khajkanda	Herb
86	Taccaceae	465	*Tacca leontopetaloides* (L.) O.Ktze.	Dukkarkand	Herb
87	Discoreaceae	466	*Dioscorea bulbifera* L.		Climber
		467	*Dioscorea pentaphylla* L.		Climber
88	Hypoxidaceae	468	*Curculigo orchioides* Gaertn.	Kali musli	Herb
89	Amaryllidaceae	469	*Crinum latifolium* L. var.latifolium		Herb
		470	*Crinum viviparum* (Lam.) R.Ansari and V.J.Nair	Nagdamni	Herb
90	Zingiberaceae	471	*Costus aromatica* Salisbs.	Kosht	Herb
		472	*Costus speciosus* (Koen.) J.E.Sm.	Kosht	Herb
		473	*Curcuma pseudomontana* Grah.	Ranhaladi	Herb
		474	*Hitchenia caulina* (Grah.) Baker in Hook.		Herb
		475	*Zingiber capitatum* Rosc.		Herb

		476	*Zingiber cernuum* Dalz.		Herb
91	Arecaceae	477	*Phoenix acaulis* Roxb.	Shevra	Shrub
92	Alismataceae	478	*Limnophyton obtusifolium* (L.) Miq.		Herb
93	Eriocaulaceae	479	*Eriocoulon dianae* Fyson in J.		Herb

Sr.No.	Family	Sr.no. plants.	Botanical Name	Common Name	Habit
94	Cyperaceae	480	*Bulbostylis barbata* (Rottb) C.B.Cl.		Herb
		481	*Cyperus articulatus* L.		Herb
		482	*Cyperus esculentus* L.		Herb
		483	*Cyperus nutans* Vahl, Enum. Var *eleusinoides*		Herb
		484	*Fuirena trilobites* C.B.Cl.		Herb
		485	*Indocourtoisia cyperoides* (Roxb.)Bennet & Raiz.		Herb
		486	*Kyllinga tenuifolia* Steud. =*Cyperus triceps*		Herb
		487	*Mariscus Cyperinus* (Retz.) Vahl, Enum.		Herb
		488	*Mariscus ferax* (L.C.Rich.) C.B.Cl.		Herb
		489	*Pycreus flavescens* (L) Reichb.		Herb
		490	*Pycreus sanguinolentus* (Vahl) Nees ex C.B.Cl.		Herb
		491	*Queenslandiella hyalina* (Vahl) Ballard.		Herb
		492	*Rikliella squarrosa* (L.) J = *Scirpus squarrosus.*		Herb
		493	*Schoenoplectus senegalensis* Raynal.		Herb
		494	*Scirpus michelianus* L.		Herb
		495	*Schoenoplectus lateriflorus* (Gmel.) Lye		Herb

Sr.No.	Family	Sr.no. plants.	Botanical Name	Common Name	Habit
95	Poaceae	496	*Dendrocalamus strictus* (Roxb.) Nees	Velu	Shrub
96	Araceae	497	*Amorphophallus bulbifera* (Roxb.) Bl.		Herb
		498	*Colocasia esculenta* (L.) Schott &Endl.	Jangali Alu	Herb
		499	*Typhonium bulbiferum* Dalz.	Cochai	Herb
97	Typhaceae	500	*Typha angustifolia* L.	Pan -kanis	Herb

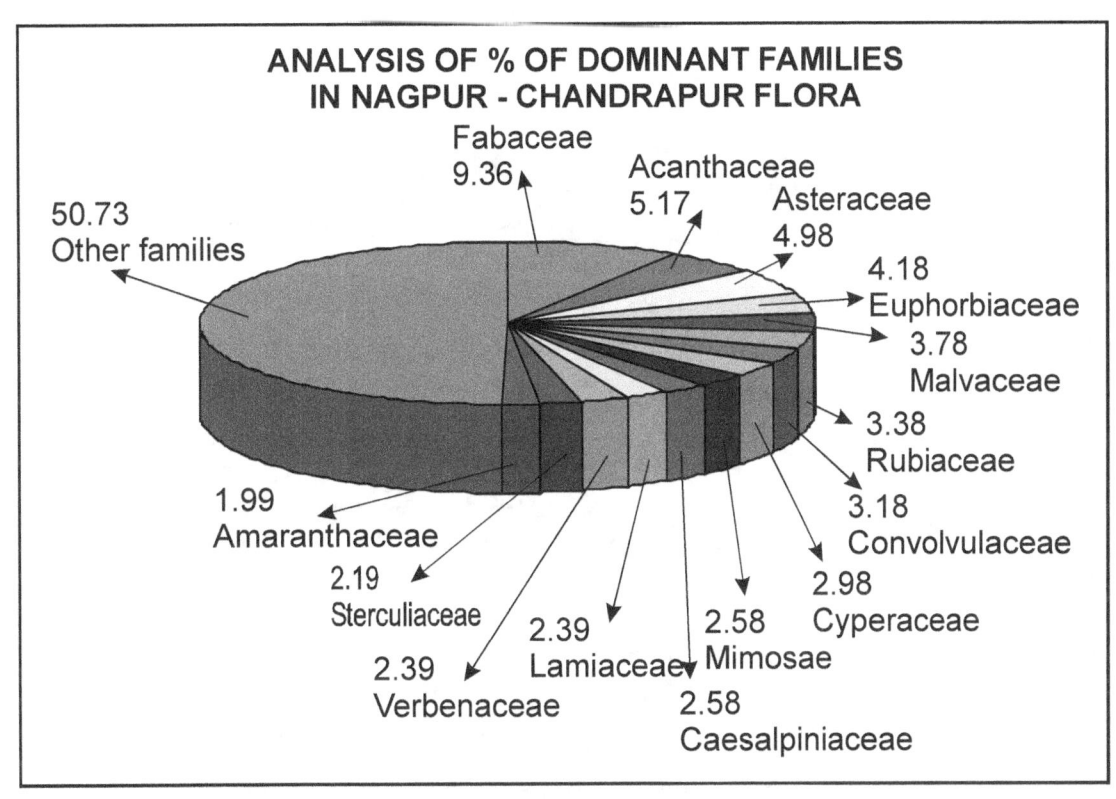

ANALYSIS OF % OF DOMINANT FAMILIES
IN NAGPUR - CHANDRAPUR FLORA

Fabaceae
9.36

Acanthaceae
5.17

Asteraceae
4.98

4.18
Euphorbiaceae

3.78
Malvaceae

3.38
Rubiaceae

3.18
Convolvulaceae

2.98
Cyperaceae

2.58
Mimosae

2.58
Caesalpiniaceae

2.39
Lamiaceae

2.39
Verbenaceae

2.19
Sterculiaceae

1.99
Amaranthaceae

50.73
Other families

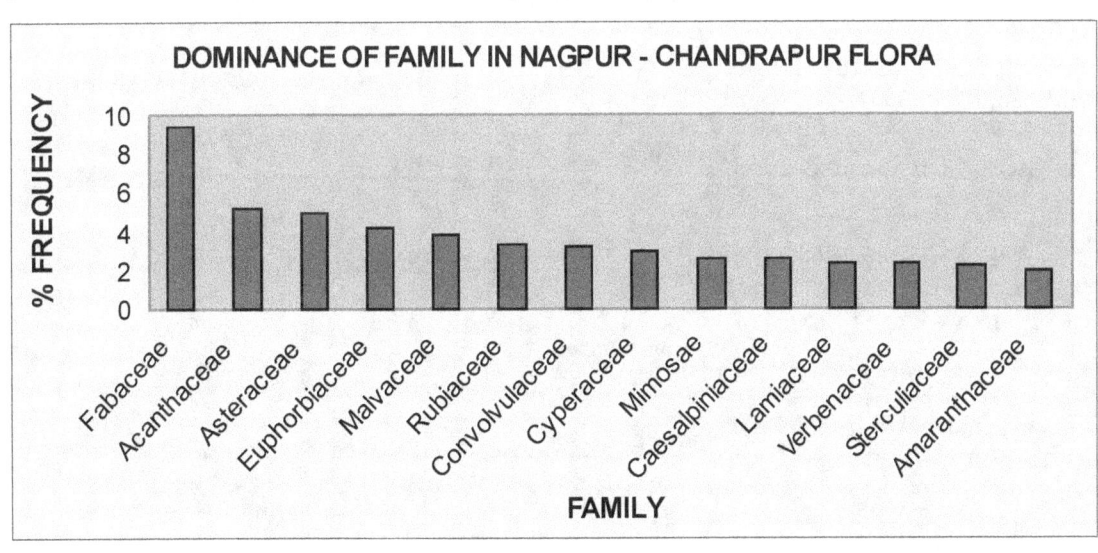

DOMINANCE OF FAMILY IN NAGPUR - CHANDRAPUR FLORA

% FREQUENCY

FAMILY

170

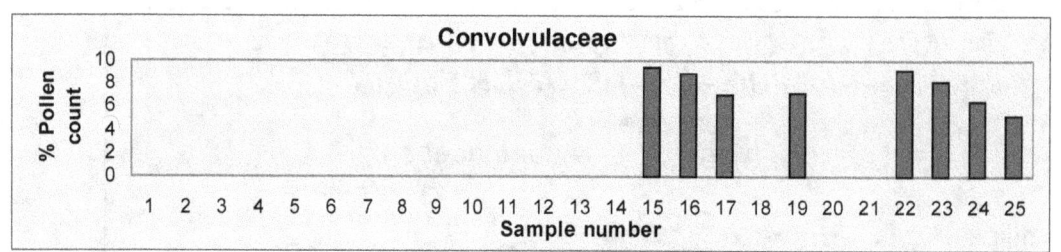

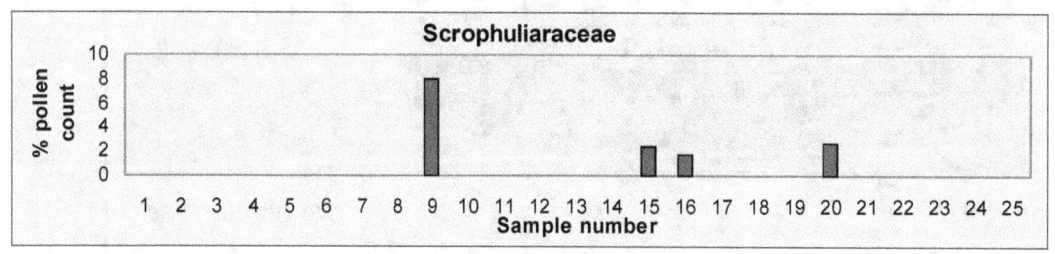

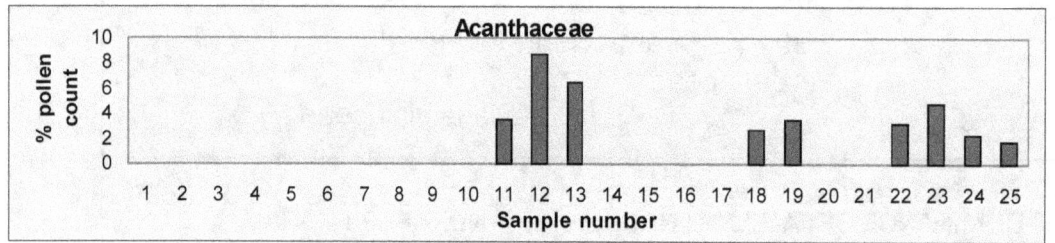

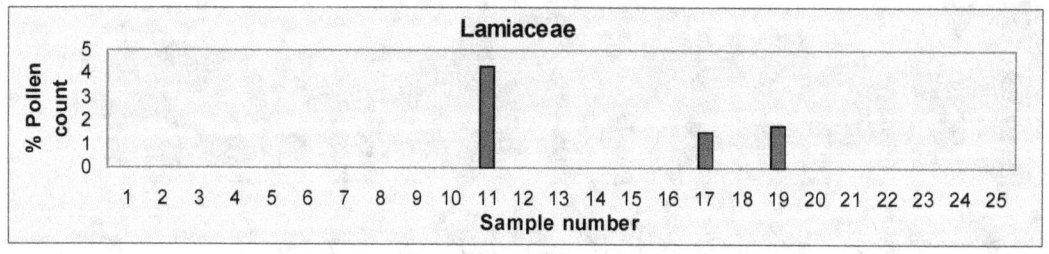

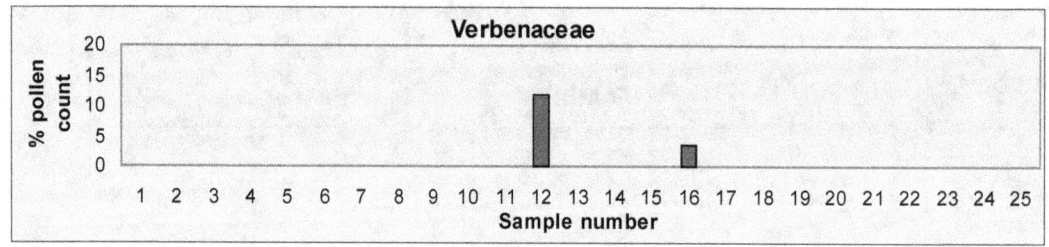

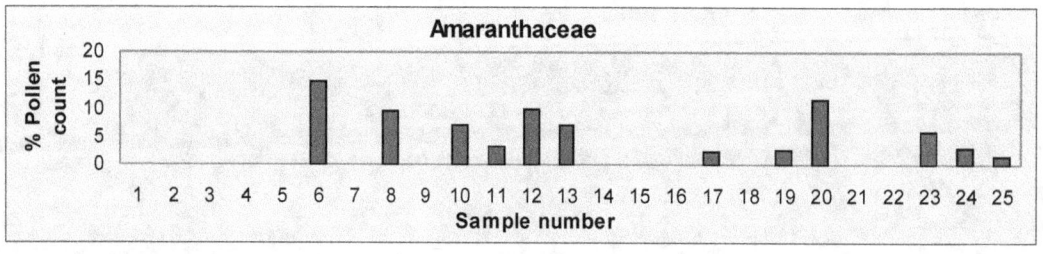

171